BEYOND PREJUDICE

This is a volume in the
Arno Press collection

THE ASIAN EXPERIENCE
IN NORTH AMERICA

Chinese and Japanese

Advisory Editor
Roger Daniels

See last pages of this volume
for a complete list of titles

Beyond Prejudice

TORU MATSUMOTO

ARNO PRESS
A New York Times Company
New York • 1978

Reprint Edition 1978 by Arno Press Inc.

Reprinted from a copy in the State Historical
    Society of Wisconsin Library

THE ASIAN EXPERIENCE IN NORTH AMERICA:
Chinese and Japanese
ISBN for complete set: 0-405-11261-0
See last pages of this volume for titles.

Manufactured in the United States of America

———————◆———————

Library of Congress Cataloging in Publication Data

Matsumoto, Toru, 1913-
    Beyond prejudice.

    (The Asian experience in North America : Chinese and
Japanese)
    Reprint of the ed. published by Friendship Press,
New York.
    Bibliography: p.
    1. Japanese Americans--Evacuation and relocation,
1942-1945. 2. Missions to Japanese--United States.
I. Title. II. Series.
D769.8.A6M35 1978   940.54'72'73   78-54826
ISBN 0-405-11283-1

Beyond Prejudice

A STORY OF THE CHURCH
AND JAPANESE AMERICANS

BY TORU MATSUMOTO

Published for

Home Missions Council of North America
Foreign Missions Conference of North America
and
Federal Council of the Churches of Christ in America
by
FRIENDSHIP PRESS
New York

TORU MATSUMOTO was born in Japan, but he is a product of East and West, having received his middle school and college education at Meiji Gakuin, a private Christian institution in Tokyo, and his theological training at Union Theological Seminary in New York. In 1944 he was ordained in New York as a minister of the Reformed Church in America.

From 1938 until the outbreak of war Mr. Matsumoto was a secretary of the Committee on Friendly Relations among Foreign Students and also general secretary of the Japanese Students' Christian Association of North America. The war and eleven months' internment interrupted his work, but late in 1942 he was released and became assistant to the executive secretary of the Committee on Resettlement of Japanese Americans, jointly sponsored by the Federal Council of Churches and the Home Missions Council of North America in cooperation with the Foreign Missions Conference of North America. From March to December, 1945, he traveled extensively as director for resettlement under the Home Missions Council, counseling with church groups on resettlement and visiting relocation centers in the interest of the churches.

Mr. Matsumoto contributes articles to church and secular magazines and is the co-author of *A Brother Is a Stranger,* published by the John Day Company.

To
TEDDY MY SON

Foreword

THE last four years have in all probability been the most disturbing years in the history of the United States and of the world. During this period we have witnessed the most revolutionary actions in the life of the nations involved in war—but no nation has been unaffected. We have become accustomed to doing things in wartime that are contradictory to Christian thinking and action, and the danger is that we may come to accept them as the normal procedure of life. This has happened within the United States of America.

The saddest chapter in the story of America's part in the war is not alone the record of the activities across the seas, but what has happened at home. Our treatment of the Japanese Americans is one of the most tragic stories in our history. Upon no other minority group in our midst have we inflicted a greater injustice in such a brief period of time. Upon a group of people whose only offense was their racial visibility we inflicted shame and suffering. We are now beginning to see the injustice of these hardships, and to seek some means of restitution. We took them from their homes without due process of the law; we put them behind barbed wire with a soldier every hundred yards to keep them in; in many instances these people lost the savings of a lifetime. We are told that this was "protective custody." This sounds more humane than a concentration camp, but have we thought of the implications? From whom were we protecting these people? From you and from me.

Well, this came to an end on December 1, 1945; the government moved all the Japanese Americans out of the relocation centers.

Now the story can be told, and Mr. Toru Matsumoto is setting it forth in this book. It is a story of sorrow and suffering, but it is also a story of triumph—the triumph of the gospel of Jesus Christ over injustice, persecution, and prejudice. It is the story of the ministry of the church to a people in their hour of trial and humiliation; a story of prejudice—yes, but as the title suggests it is a story "beyond prejudice."

This story will remain for all time as a record of the unselfish service of the church. It is a story of the one shining star in a black, black sky, but we thank God for this one shining star and take courage. We wish for this book the widest possible reading within the church. It should mean much to the church as it seeks to re-establish the Christian mission in Japan, but it also should mean much to the church at home.

The writing of this book has been encouraged, and the publication is being sponsored, by a joint committee representing the East Asia Committee of the Foreign Missions Conference of North America, the Committee on Japanese Work of the Home Missions Council of North America, and the Federal Council of Churches.

New York City,   MARK A. DAWBER.
May, 1946.

Contents

Acknowledgment

In preparing the manuscript for this book, I have received letters and other original materials amounting to more than one thousand pages, both in English and in Japanese, from almost one hundred persons. To each one of them I owe a personal debt. I regret that lack of space makes it impossible to mention their names.

For the encouragement to write this story I thank Dr. Luman J. Shafer, Mr. Joe J. Mickle, and Dr. Mark A. Dawber. For their constructive criticisms of the contents, my appreciation is due Dr. Roswell P. Barnes and Dr. J. Quinter Miller. I am also indebted to Dr. Willis G. Hoekje and Mr. George B. Ahn, Jr., for their painstaking editorial assistance, and to Mrs. Margaret Reynolds and Mrs. Gertrude Rutherford for their hard labor in typing the manuscript.

The War Relocation Authority deserves credit for many data supplied. For their assistance given me at the time of my tour of the relocation centers, I thank both my evacuee friends and the W.R.A. personnel.

T. M.

Introduction

SUDDEN as an earthquake, the outbreak of war with Japan shook Japanese communities in America. The tidal waves of hysteria and fear that followed swept every Japanese and Japanese American away from the Pacific Coast region to an ocean of confusion and exile. Never before in the history of the United States had a whole section of the population been uprooted from their homes and taken away to camps, solely on the basis of racial ancestry. It happened here in the spring of 1942, when the entire population of Japanese descent on the West Coast, 110,000 persons in all, were evacuated from their homes by military order and sent to relocation centers.

On December 7, 1941, Japan attacked the United States at Pearl Harbor, on Oahu in the Hawaii group. The next day Congress declared war on Japan. As the black smoke of the destruction in Hawaii spread over the skies of America, the public, angered at Japan, focused suspicious attention on the Japanese in America as a potential Fifth Column. "They must have known; they must have helped . . . ."

Apprehensive lest a single deed of violence against the Japanese might touch off mob hysteria, the Attorney General urged the nation on December 8 not to treat all persons of Japanese extraction indiscriminately. "There are many whose loyalty, even in the present emergency, is unquestioned," he declared.

The Federal Bureau of Investigation went to work at

once. Germany and Italy declared war against the United States, and their nationals, as well as Japanese, whom the Bureau considered potentially dangerous, were arrested and placed in custody, until their loyalty could be ascertained by hearing boards. The total thus apprehended reached several thousand people throughout the country.

The Attorney General also assured the nation that there was no sabotage in Hawaii at the time of the attack. But irresponsible rumors spread unchecked. A clamor for the mass removal of all Japanese, both citizens and aliens, arose from several sources on the Pacific Coast, such as the Joint Committee on Oriental Immigration and the Native Sons and Daughters of the Golden State.

On February 13, 1942, a letter was addressed to the President by the Pacific Coast Congressional delegation recommending evacuation, despite the absence of hysteria or signs of mob violence. The Japanese on the coast pulled down the shades in their homes, waiting uneasily for what the government would do.

Then, on February 19, 1942, the President issued an executive order authorizing the Secretary of War, or designated military commanders, to prescribe military areas from which "any or all" persons might be excluded, or in which their movements might be restricted. And citizens and aliens of Japanese ancestry were classified as more dangerous than aliens of Italian or German descent. Those who could move were urged to go to the interior voluntarily.

In February the House Committee on National Defense Migration, headed by Congressman John H. Tolan, began hearings on the Pacific Coast regarding enemy aliens and others in that area. The committee's main purpose was to determine whether or not a proposed mass evacuation of all Japanese, regardless of citizenship, was necessary.

On March 2, Lieutenant General John L. DeWitt, commanding general of the Western Defense Command created the Wartime Civil Control Administration (W.C.C.A.) to supervise the evacuation. Work on assembly centers began. On March 18, the War Relocation Authority (W.R.A.), a civilian agency, was created by the President to succeed W.C.C.A., to plan and carry out an orderly relocation. Mr. Milton S. Eisenhower, of the Department of Agriculture, was appointed director of the W.R.A. Voluntary evacuation was found impractical and even dangerous. When the W.R.A. consulted a group of governors of western states, all but one refused to guarantee order and safety for relocating Japanese and Japanese Americans. The governor of Colorado was the exception. He said, "If we do not extend humanity's kindness and understanding to these people . . . we are tearing down the whole American system."

On March 23, the first contingent of one thousand, all persons of Japanese ancestry, left Los Angeles voluntarily for the reception center at Manzanar, California, to prepare it as a temporary residence for evacuees assigned to it.

Then came the curfew order, requiring German and Italian aliens and all citizens and aliens of Japanese ancestry to stay at home from 8 P.M. to 6 A.M., and prohibiting travel of more than five miles from home without a permit.

The first evacuation to an assembly center took place from Bainbridge Island, Washington; the second from Terminal Island, California. The first phase of the total movement was completed by June, 1942. Meanwhile, the next phase —movement to relocation centers—got under way.

Altogether ten relocation centers, which were to become "homes" for 106,775 evacuees, were established. They were:

Name	Location	Population as of Jan., 1943
Central Utah	Topaz, Utah	7,910
Colorado River	Poston, Arizona	17,620
Gila River	Rivers, Arizona	13,341
Granada	Amache, Colorado	6,822
Heart Mountain	Heart Mountain, Wyoming	10,721
Jerome	Denson, Arkansas	7,817
Manzanar	Manzanar, California	9,916
Minidoka	Hunt, Idaho	9,091
Rohwer	McGehee, Arkansas	8,447
Tule Lake	Newell, California	15,090
		106,775

By November, 1942, all relocation to these centers had been accomplished, *without untoward incident.*

How was it possible that the whole group, two-thirds of them American citizens, against whom no charge of crime had been lodged by the government, had been able to comply with the most drastic requirement that our government has ever applied to any such group, quite without incident?

Again, when selective service was halted among the Japanese Americans after the evacuation, what happened? Hundreds volunteered for combat service, and were enrolled in an all-Japanese American unit, which won the Presidential Unit citation twice and became one of the most decorated units in the history of the United States Army.

There is no group of citizens that has borne more mental and economic hardship during this war than the Japanese Americans. Still, they have kept their integrity and loyalty.

Any attempt to explain the wartime record of our Japanese Americans is superfluous. But two factors seem to warrant our special attention: the characteristic sense of responsibility and discipline of the Japanese American leadership, particularly of the Christian group; and the sense of justice on the part of fair-minded Americans—Christians many of them, taking their Christianity seriously.

The way the churches have risen above the hysteria of war and rendered services to the evacuee is a story of which Christians in America can be proud. True, not all churches or individual Christians have stood on the side of justice and brotherhood. But if it had not been for the tireless efforts of those, both inside and outside the Japanese group, who kept the Christian sense of responsibility in the critical periods of mass evacuation and resettlement, the problem created by the unprecedented action of the government would have remained largely unsolved.

With the return of peace, the Christian churches in the United States face a rare opportunity and heavy responsibility for healing the wounds of mankind. In facing them, Christians shall do well to remember how the churches have met their opportunity and discharged their responsibility with regard to Japanese Americans. For the Christians of ethnic minorities in America and the younger churches in the East the story of the church and Japanese Americans will be a matter of deep interest.

The chapters that follow tell the story, in substance if not in full detail. It is the story of how the church and the Japanese Americans have tried to solve their great problem—together.

Explanation

A word of explanation is in order lest the reader think that this is a report on the work of the church for Japanese Americans during the war just ended. This is *a* story, and not the *whole* story, of the church and Japanese Americans. For this reason, many individuals and groups that have played important parts in the whole story and therefore should be spoken of in a comprehensive report are not mentioned in this book. To mention them would have required several hundred pages. The choice of narrators and characters appearing in the story was made upon my own responsibility based on their representative qualities, and not necessarily upon their prominence in the drama.

Furthermore, my choice of the subject was not motivated by any desire to claim all the credit for the church. I happened to specialize in the services of the church during the war. Through official and unofficial contacts with non-church agencies, however, I learned a great deal about their work. Their contribution should not be forgotten, but I am not competent to write about it.

T. M.

1

From the Pioneers to the Evacuation

THE first Japanese church in America was born in the basement of a Chinese church in San Francisco in 1877. A few students from Japan and a Christian American woman, with the help of the Methodist Episcopal mission to the Chinese, were God's instruments in the beginning of a movement that was to grow thirty, sixty, even one hundred fold within the short period of fifty years.

The students were already Christian. The work of the Protestant missions in Japan had yielded results, though that work had been started less than two decades before. For the people of nineteenth-century Japan, conversion to Christianity was a complete departure from the past—the past of isolation, while the country had been closed to the rest of the world for about two hundred and fifty years. When the country was opened and Christianity was reintroduced after being suppressed under the penalty of death for so long, it gave to those who accepted it a complete *new* way of life—almost too radically new and alien. But the youth who were touched by the dynamic meaning of Christianity cast off the shell of social tradition and personal security, and became fervent evangelists. Thus the modest mission that began its work in an abandoned Buddhist temple in Yokohama produced as first fruits Japanese Christians who turned to the task of evangelizing their own people.

A few of these had now crossed the Pacific Ocean to "the country from which missionaries came." A few hundreds of their fellow countrymen had preceded them.

Speaking about the first immigrants from Japan a veteran Japanese minister, the Reverend Mr. Seizo Abe, says, "Those youths of Japan, their lungs filled with the air of a new freedom, their hearts burning with enthusiasm for democracy, left their country, which had just opened her doors to the world. They were eager to learn new ways of life. They also dreamed of golden opportunities beyond the seas."

For the churches of America, the coming of these people was a new opportunity. Since there already were missions to the Chinese on the West Coast, it was natural that the churches should begin their work among the Japanese almost as soon as they set their feet on American soil.

In the words of Mr. Abe again, "The first to ex.end a hand of welcome to them were the Christian churches on the coast. The mission buildings of the churches became hostels for the newcomers. They also functioned as schools of English and of American customs, and later as clearing houses for employment."

The church in the basement was the first of these. This first church, though split into three groups by the administrative differences among the sponsoring bodies, provided the norm for all later churches, in that leadership responsibility was borne largely by the Japanese.

Another important characteristic of the Japanese church work was the evangelistic zeal of its leaders. That the mission premises served as centers of orientation to American life as well as social centers was secondary in importance.

Immigration from Japan reached its high mark at the

turn of the century. Of twenty-five thousand Japanese then in America, twelve thousand were migrants by way of Hawaii. The Japanese were first welcomed as needed manpower, but as their number increased they inherited the antiforeign sentiment which had been shown to Chinese. Yet the churches' fostering care grew in scope as the people spread along the coast, and by the time the immigration stopped completely in 1924 upon the passing of the Oriental Exclusion Law, there were forty Japanese churches in California, one in Oregon, seven in Washington, two each in Utah and Colorado, and four in New York. Other types of religious work were also established in the intermountain region, eastern Washington, Nebraska, Chicago, and Boston. Denominations having missions, and some of them sister churches in Japan, were easily led to minister to Japanese here.

The churches having Japanese work in America through these years included the Methodist Episcopal, the Presbyterian (North), the Congregational, the Baptist, the Society of Friends, the Protestant Episcopal, the Christian (Disciples), the Nazarene, the Holiness, the Free Methodist, the Reformed in America (Dutch). The Salvation Army, the Y.M.C.A., and the Y.W.C.A. also entered the field.

As the work thus spread with many groups participating, a common desire was felt by American workers to coordinate all these missions. Under the initiative of the Home Missions Council such a coordinating arrangement was inaugurated, but not without the usual difficulty. There was some denominational overlapping even though comity arrangements had been agreed upon in the several areas.

Among the Japanese Christians and their able leadership,

2

to whom the American churches ministered, there was a strong desire for cooperation. But if the zeal for cooperation among American workers was for the purpose of coordination, this desire among the Japanese was mostly for the sake of their own growth in independence and self-discipline. However, they aimed at perfection and their cooperative efforts collapsed under the weight of over-organization. Nevertheless, strong Japanese church federations existed in northern and southern California. Voluntary cooperation among the Japanese churches was also especially noteworthy, a factor that later proved invaluable for a cooperative program in the relocation centers.

One important reason for the rapid growth in number of the Japanese churches was the fact that trained leaders were readily available from the theological schools in Japan, which had been supported largely by the American churches. America's "foreign" missionaries were among their teachers. How conclusive a proof this is that "foreign" and "home" missions of the church are one and inseparable!

These imported Japanese ministers showed not only zeal for preaching, but also a remarkable ability for evangelism by literature. To say that this use of literature was forced upon them because the people were scattered is to overlook Japanese emphasis upon the power of written words. The Japanese are a reading people, and the ministers were excellent writers. Thus, besides weekly bulletins of individual churches, there was an interdenominational paper called *The New Heaven and Earth.* Lack of funds necessitated the suspension of this useful publication, however.

Japanese Christians were also keenly conscious of their responsibility among their own people. They faced a problem of moral degeneration within the Japanese community as it became influenced by the larger community around it, though the former was isolated from the latter socially. At the same time, that larger community was becoming increasingly hostile. These problems had to be attacked: low moral conduct was unchristian, therefore a challenge; isolation was against the spirit of the Christian church; discrimination was unchristian, undemocratic, and un-American, and it had to be met.

Against the corruption among their fellow compatriots, the Japanese Christians plunged into a direct and aggressive campaign of wiping out evil practices, such as gambling and prostitution. Ministers and lay leaders of all denominations were united in this effort. In addition, since these two particular vices were well entrenched in the neighboring Chinese communities, Chinese and Japanese churches worked together. Ringleaders of gambling and prostitution were identified, and some of them were sent back to Japan. This campaign was aggressively carried out, but the progress made was purchased with sacrifice in lives. The first Japanese Christian martyr on the West Coast was assassinated during this campaign.

The almost complete absence of juvenile delinquency among the Orientals on the West Coast was largely due to the constant self-discipline of families and the fine moral leadership of the religious and civic organizations of our Oriental residents.

To overcome the hostility towards the Japanese seemed a mammoth task. First of all, it was a part of the general anti-Orientalism, with its long history dating back to the first coming of the Chinese laborers. Roots of antagonism were deep, for they were economic, social, emotional, and, more lately, political. The passing of the Exclusion Law was the decisive turning point in the life of the Japanese in America.

American Christians in Japan protested against the Exclusion Law, but with no results. Japanese Christians in America received a crushing blow and felt that all their good labor was lost and gone. Christian churches of America were represented by the Federal Council of the Churches of Christ in America in the campaign against the bill, but the efforts ended unsuccessfully. The enactment of the law did not tend to reduce anti-Japanese sentiment; on the contrary, it steadily increased, receiving new impetus from public disapproval of Japan's actions in the Far East.

What were Japanese Christians to do? Despite their unanimity of opinion that they must represent the best the Japanese could be, there were differences as to their approaches to the subject. Some undertook to improve the relationship between the Japanese and others on the West Coast by means of a better understanding on an individual basis. This group tended to stimulate a progressive assimilation of the Japanese, especially the American-born children, in the general community. Others felt that a better understanding between Japan and the United States was more important and immediate.

Largely because of the total stoppage in immigration after 1924, and the frustration suffered in the passing of the Exclusion Law, there was a period of inaction among the Japanese churches as far as their intercourse with the general community was concerned. It was not until the American-born children grew old enough to be noticed that the

American churches took more cognizance of Japanese churches. In fact, the general indifference of Christian leaders of America to the problems of the Orientals during this period was one of the causes of the segregation of the Japanese and others of Oriental background on the West Coast. Not only that, but underlying forces and attitudes that later contributed to the evacuation of the Japanese from the West Coast were almost entirely disregarded by American church leaders. Only in isolated cases did individuals who felt concern try their best to bring the young Japanese Americans into a fellowship with Caucasian Christian youths. In Pismo Beach, California, where there was no segregated church, a considerable number of Japanese Christians had become active members in American churches, thus showing that, when given an opportunity, Japanese were capable of identifying themselves fully with Americans. Student Christian movements of the West Coast regions did the best work along this line.

This, however, did not solve the problem of the children of the first-generation Japanese. They were Americans. Nothing that the older generation did, out of their sympathy for Japan, should jeopardize the future of these young Americans who were growing up with the rest of Americans in speech, manner, and ideas. The American children of Japanese parents had their future in America, and in America alone. There was no question or argument about it. Was it not better, then, that the older people, who would be aliens as long as they lived, consider themselves "parents of American citizens" and act accordingly?

This was the argument for Japanese parents to become as American as possible, and helped the new program of the church. For the churches had begun training the Nisei (the second generation) to assume responsibility and leadership. If the Nisei grew up not only as Americans but also as Christians, church leaders felt, these young Americans in spite of their Oriental faces could walk the streets of America with confidence in themselves. Most notable efforts along this line were the annual Northern and Southern California Young People's Christian Conferences held under inter-church auspices, which attracted large numbers of Nisei Christians. Japanese churches began to grow again. Boards of the interested denominations assisted in training Nisei ministers or invited young Japanese theological students who had come here to study to remain in America and minister to the Nisei in English. As for the Issei (the first generation), the churches' ultimate obligation to them was to provide spiritual consolation at all times. Even if all human efforts failed to improve their lot, God would never desert them. In their faith in God, therefore, they rested their future. Meanwhile the clouds of war gathered ominously over the Pacific.

That no Issei seriously expected that the country of his birth and the country of his adoption would come to a violent clash of arms was evidenced by complete absence of preparation on the part of the West Coast Japanese for the catastrophe that did befall them. As for the Nisei, they were confident that even if their country fought Japan, their rights and obligations as American citizens would not be treated any differently from those of all other American citizens. Japanese Christian churches typified this general attitude of "business as usual."

First surprise, then consternation, but finally composure

characterized the Japanese Christians on the day Japan attacked Pearl Harbor. Their reactions have been told by many Nisei ministers. One of them, the Reverend Thomas J. Machida, minister of the Seattle Japanese Methodist Church, wrote:

December 7 was Sunday and we held our usual Issei and Nisei combined worship services at our church. There were about three hundred worshipers present. In the afternoon, we held our monthly Ladies' Aid Society meeting. During the services, at about four o'clock, a lady came rushing to the church and said that she had just heard a peculiar broadcast over the radio that bombing planes with the rising sun insignia had attacked the Hawaiian Islands. No one could believe it. When we went home and turned our own radios on, we clearly heard voices from Hawaii confirming it.

The thought, "Why did Japan do that?" flashed into our minds. That night, I had a speaking engagement at the West Seattle Methodist Church. I was rather undecided for a while as to whether I should go and preach to the American congregation. I decided that I should do it under any circumstances, and I drove my car to the church and did my part as though nothing had happened. The congregation listened so intently that the drop of a pin could be heard. I was well received by them afterwards. I talked on the theme "Walking in the Light with Christian Brotherhood."

The arrest of thousands of Japanese aliens by the agents of the Federal Bureau of Investigation began that night and continued for several weeks. It was usually the heads of families who were leaders in the Japanese community who were taken away from their homes. This alone was sufficient to throw the whole Japanese group into utter confusion and fear. But to make it worse, the scare headlines in the newspapers placed both the Issei and Nisei in a peculiarly vulnerable position for attack and suspicion.

Two days later, the Federal Council of the Churches of Christ in America, the Foreign Missions Conference of North America, and the Home Missions Council of North America, through their respective presidents, issued a joint appeal to the American people.

Under the emotional strain of the moment, Americans will be tempted to express their resentment against the action of Japan's government by recriminations against the Japanese people who are in our midst. We are gratified to observe that the agents of our government are dealing with them with consideration.

Let us remember that many of these people are loyal, patriotic American citizens and that others, though Japanese subjects, have been utterly opposed to their nation's acts against our nation. It is incumbent upon us to demonstrate a discipline which, while carefully observing the precautions necessary to national safety, has no place for vindictiveness.

We, therefore, call upon the church people of this country to maintain a Christian composure and charity in their dealings with the Japanese among us.

Signed: LUTHER A. WEIGLE
SUE E. WEDDELL
G. PITT BEERS

Among the Japanese, their Christian churches provided the main steadying influence. American churches also sprang to action. But until the direction of the policy of the government was clarified, there was no end to the confusion and despair.

What the Christians in the Pacific northwest area did in those uncertain days is recalled by the Reverend Everett W. Thompson, a former missionary in Japan under the Methodist board, who was then serving the Japanese Methodist Church in Seattle. He wrote:

Pastors of Caucasian churches and Caucasian neighbors and friends shared with the pastors of the Japanese churches in trying to meet the needs which grew out of this situation. In a few cases, we were present when an arrest was made and were able to help as interpreters. In many more, we called at the home shortly afterward to reassure the family that such an arrest was not a disgrace and that we had all confidence in the integrity of the arrested man. Next, calls were made on the men themselves in the local jail, and even several hundred miles away at the camps where they were being kept. They had no formal trial; they were accused of no specific charge. They eventually had hearings to see if certain suspicions against them were properly justified.

In many of these hearings, church leaders with a knowledge of Japanese—most of them former missionaries in Japan—took part. But long before even the first of this long-drawn-out series of hearings was held, other pressing problems had to be faced back home. There were the business problems arising out of the man's absence and the problems of family income. There were complicated arrangements to be worked out so that the business might go on. Many pastors and church workers had a share in arranging bank accounts or guaranteeing people now under suspicion because the FBI had taken their husbands or fathers, or merely translating and interpreting in business arrangements. Sometimes all that one could do was to make a friendly call. Welfare agencies had to be appealed to to provide financial assistance till the father could return. Then there were people who needed extension of their restricted travel permits, and people for whom emergency tasks had to be performed after the restrictive curfew hours.

The churches also immediately took two lines of action to deal with the general emergency: (1) Christian grocers donated for relief what they felt they could not sell; and the Japanese churches immediately bought through Caucasian workers small supplies of groceries for immediate distribution where most desperately needed. The pastors were in touch with practically all their people. Interested lay workers brought word of distress to the pastors. One Japanese American grocer put his entire stock of food at the disposal of his pastor. (2) Caucasian workers in Japanese churches brought this problem promptly to the attention of the Seattle Council of Churches, which telegraphed to Washington and almost immediately received a reply in the form of an official pronouncement in all the newspapers lifting most of the restrictions from personal dealings, and from small businesses owned by residents in America.

In southern California, according to the Reverend and Mrs. Royden Susu-Mago, of the Japanese Independent Church in Hollywood, the churches began to make their influence felt. Individual pastors, like the Reverend Allan A. Hunter of Mt. Hollywood Congregational Church, used their influence to have Japanese of their acquaintance freed from FBI detention, particularly in some cases where they had been detained on far-fetched charges.

Ministers played a unique rôle in other ways. For example, an American couple whose son had been killed at Pearl Harbor went to their pastor for help, asking his prayers. After praying together, they went away comforted; but before long, they were back again in need of more reassurance. When this had happened several times, the minister decided that something more than prayer was needed; that the answer to this couple's grief lay in positive service. The next time they came to him, he ventured to tell them of a loyal Japanese family in the neighborhood who had suffered much since war began and who were sadly in need of a friend.

The Caucasian couple could not rise to this. They went away still wrapped in their sorrow and burdened with a new grief that their pastor could prove so lacking in understanding as to propose that they—whose son had been killed by the Japanese—stretch out the hand of fellowship to the enemy at home! But before a week had passed, they were back to learn the name and address of the Japanese family.

The Reverend Lester E. Suzuki, pastor of the Japanese Methodist Church in Los Angeles, reported: "I wrote a general letter to many churches telling of the situation among our people. Immediately, churches and individuals began sending money for the relief of the needy families. This fund we distributed among the families whose heads were being detained by the government and had no means of livelihood. County welfare had too many technicalities to facilitate the relief of these helpless families."

Rumors of sabotage by Japanese in Hawaii were headlined in the West Coast papers. A Japanese submarine shelled Santa Barbara. A few Japanese were bodily harmed by hoodlums. All this gave support to a demand that all Japanese be cleared from the entire West Coast, either by interning them or sending them elsewhere. Denials by the government of Japanese sabotage in Hawaii were not given the public until much later.

During this period of uncertainty and confusion, Caucasian superintendents and field representatives of the denominations having work among the Japanese were in constant touch with each other. Dr. Frank Herron Smith, superintendent of the Japanese Methodist churches, who had been most closely associated with the Japanese, took initiative in coordinating the church workers' efforts to help the Japanese.

Just about this time Dr. Mark A. Dawber, executive secretary of the Home Missions Council, hurried to the West Coast and met with the group called by Dr. Smith, and in the name of the Commission on Aliens and Prisoners of War, created jointly by the Federal Council of Churches and the Home Missions Council, commissioned them to serve the Japanese by assisting Japanese churches, regardless of denomination. Thus the Protestant Church Commission for Japanese Service was inaugurated, with headquarters in San Francisco. The Reverend Gordon K. Chapman, formerly a Presbyterian missionary in Japan, was named executive secretary.

As for the controversy about the Japanese, President Roosevelt ended it by authorizing the Army to control their life and movements in the interest of national security.

Dr. Smith was one of many who wrote to General John L. DeWitt, the Western Defense Commander, "urging selective evacuation and offering the services of eighty returned missionaries and reliable Japanese as interpreters."

On February 27, Dr. Smith, Mr. Chapman, Mr. Galen M. Fisher, a former Y.M.C.A. secretary in Japan and friend of the Nisei, Mr. W. C. James, a Friend and business man in Berkeley, California, and Dr. C. A. Richardson, a secretary of the Methodist board in New York, called on General DeWitt. But he refused to meet them, and instead named Colonel Magill, provost marshal, as his substitute. To him and to Colonel Weed, chief chaplain, they presented a plea not to evacuate all Japanese, citizens and aliens alike, as it was rumored was to be done, but rather to "screen" the Japanese communities by individual hearings. Church buildings and interpreters were offered for this purpose.

Meanwhile, Congress sent the Honorable John H. Tolan, chairman of the House Defense Migration Investigating Committee, to the West Coast for the purpose of conducting hearings on the proposed total evacuation. Dr. Smith said:

Mr. Tolan was a college classmate of mine, so it was not difficult to secure places on the hearing program for Protestant representatives at San Francisco, Los Angeles, Portland, and Seattle. In each place, we stood for the principle of selective evacuation with hearings for the suspects, as contrasted with the proposed plan for mass evacuation. On February 23, a panel was held in San Francisco. Dr. Paul Reagor, president of the Northern California Church Federation, was the first speaker. He was supported by the Messrs. Chapman, Fisher, James, and myself. At Los Angeles, the president of the Federation of Southern California was "too busy," so the chief statement was made by Dr. F. W. Heckelman, supported by Bishop James C. Baker, of the Methodist Church, and Dr. E. C. Farnham of the Los Angeles Federation. The Portland Council of Churches declined to testify at a Tolan hearing. The representation was made by Miss Azalia E. Peet, a returned missionary, supported by Methodist Bishop Bruce R. Baxter. At Seattle, the Church Federation stood the test and the chief speaker was Dr. Harold Jensen, the president. In these hearings the church representatives, the CIO, and, in some instances, the Japanese American Citizens League, were the only champions for fair treatment of the Japanese.

These efforts, however, did not avail. General DeWitt ordered a mass evacuation.

Mr. Thompson of Seattle observed that one very large reason why there was not more bitterness and sense of frustration in the face of flagrant injustice was the constant steadying influence of the Japanese churches in sermon, worship service, discussion group, and pastoral calling.

When the blow fell and the official announcement was made that all Japanese and Japanese Americans were to be removed beyond a line some one hundred to one hundred and fifty miles from the coast every family had a number of difficult personal problems to solve. What of students about to begin their college education? Could they be transferred elsewhere? What should one do with a business necessarily tied to one spot, one group of customers—sell out in a hurry at a sharp loss? How long was one going to be away—a few months or forever? How about furniture— sell, store, or lend it? And one's own house—sell or let it? All these problems were difficult. But the decision had to be made in a hurry. Often no one but the person concerned could do much about it. But in the storage of furniture, the churches were able to be of real assistance. While the government later offered storage space, day by day the time of departure grew closer and yet no suitable places were announced. So the Japanese churches opened their buildings for storage of furniture for members and their friends.

The order for the evacuation announced on February 19, 1942, at first permitted voluntary and individual exodus from the prescribed areas. A few thousand people responded and started eastward. But soon it became dangerous for persons with Japanese faces to travel, as signs of active hostility appeared along the routes of evacuation.

Consequently, on March 27, 1942, the voluntary system was stopped. The people were given the freezing and curfew orders and they awaited their turns to assemble at designated places for transfer to other designated places.

One of the most hectic evacuation experiences, as told by the Susu-Magos, was that on Terminal Island near Los

Angeles, where the people were ordered to move out within a month. Suddenly the month was shortened to twenty-four hours! Twenty-four hours in which to dispose of real estate, boats, nets, household goods and pets, and to pack clothing, bedding, and the few necessities for camp life that would be permitted evacuees! The Los Angeles Church Federation stepped in and was able to have the twenty-four hours extended to forty-eight.

Most of the men at Terminal Island had been arrested by the FBI, this being the fishing village that was supposed to harbor a spy ring. A blackout was in effect and the Japanese were not permitted the use of flashlights or other "signaling devices." Confusion piled upon confusion. Twenty miles away in Los Angeles, the Japanese Church Federation met in a desperate effort to plan help for the people at Terminal Island. Where could they get trucks and drivers to evacuate them? Where could they be taken for temporary shelter, since none of the assembly centers were ready? Fortunately, the Federation succeeded in arranging sleeping quarters in various school and church properties in Los Angeles.

Meanwhile, with the forty-eight hours rapidly melting away, Caucasian ministers and laymen rushed their cars, trucks, and flashlights to Terminal Island. A Baptist pastor did his best to care for all the members of the Japanese Baptist Church there. The Reverend Herbert Nicholson of the Friends Church borrowed a truck and made several trips to the city during the night, never pausing to ask the church affiliation of those he helped. Mr. Joe Moody of the Congregational Christian Church led the twelve-truck fleet from his mattress factory to the harbor and kept the trucks running as long as they were needed. Others stayed through the night, helping with the loading and the packing, or holding flashlights. Thus Terminal Island was evacuated of Japanese but with heavy losses to the evacuees through the forced sale of valuable possessions: cars, refrigerators, pianos, and household furnishings.

In Portland, Oregon, an active committee, with headquarters in the city Y.W.C.A., representing Baptist, Episcopal, and Methodist churches, the Japanese American Citizens League, and the Y.W.C.A. met frequently and acted as a "clearing house" for problems concerning the Japanese. Miss Mildred Bartholomew of the Y.W.C.A. tells a touching story of a child in those days of fears and tears. Confronted with the phrase "enemy alien" as applied to her mother, who was born in Japan, the child said to her mother when she came home from school,

"Mommie, you are my enemy."

"Yes, darling, but Jesus said you should love your enemy," said the mother.

The little girl replied as she flew into her mother's arms, "I do, Mommie, I do!"

In the Bay region, California, churches were organized to help the evacuees with numerous problems. Miss Eleanor Breed of the First Congregational Church in San Francisco tells a moving story of day-to-day happenings around a church where she worked. Her church had been designated as one of the registration centers where the evacuees were required to report in person to give information about themselves in preparation for the evacuation. As soon as the news of this service was broadcast, many people telephoned the church to offer their help or to inquire what the church was doing. Miss Breed tells the story of those days as follows:

Soldiers were stationed around the building. They were very considerate of the Japanese, I noticed, treating them like human beings. Good old America! I was pleased.

Then, there was the couple who had a Japanese gardener, who came to them to say that he could not work that day. He had to go to the church to register. "You know," he told them, "they are going to serve tea. It is the only church in the state of California that is serving tea to the Japanese." My friends hastened to claim membership in this wonderful church and said they could see their stock rise in his estimation.

Tuesday, April 28, the beginning of the evacuation. The pioneer group of evacuees was waiting at the church in the morning. The W.C.C.A. office had lists posted around its walls saying who was to go when, and many Japanese came to read. Among the first group was a pair of newlyweds, arm in arm, the bride with a collegiate bandana around her head and a flower in her pompadour, and a big American flag in brilliants on her lapel. There were also two babies in baskets, a three-weeks-old little girl and a six-months-old boy. And everyone, young, middle-aged and old, wore a tag around his neck or hanging from his lapel with his name printed on and a number for his family group. One pert little college girl in slacks had her name tag around her neck, tied to a chain from which dangled her Phi Beta Kappa key.

The preliminary group was a small one. Their duffle bags were loaded into the big bus, and the evacuees went aboard, singing merrily and cracking jokes with their friends who were to follow within the next few days. But as the bus pulled out, a Nisei girl was crying.

A Japanese young man came to the office and said, "Would you mind if I left the church a small donation? We appreciate very much what you are doing."

"Goodness," I said, "what we are doing is only a small thing —we'd like to do more. We'd be happier if you would save

3

your donation for some play equipment for the children when you get to camp."

The man smiled. "We appreciate what your church has done," he said again, adding as an afterthought, "I'm a Buddhist."

Dean Monroe E. Deutsch of the University of California wrote us today:

"Allow me to express my own appreciation for the attitude which you and your church have taken with reference to the Japanese and the American Japanese who are being evacuated. Your action has been one that is proper and will impress these people with the fact that the ideals which we profess we try to put into practice. If any criticize you for it, my only thought would be that they are not truly Christians.

"People fail to recall that these people who are being evacuated have had no charges against them individually; they are not guilty of misconduct. They are being removed because of fear, which is gripping the hearts of some people. Personally, I feel that our country will some day feel ashamed of its conduct in this entire matter. In the meantime, however, it is good to know of actions such as you and the members of your church have taken."

Another picture to remember: the young Chinese woman told me a story . . . citing one Japanese who was a veteran of the first World War and who was removed from his successful shop in Chinatown and sent into camp as if he were a suspect.

"The fact that he came here to an American church and was given friendly treatment," she said, "helped a lot to soften his hurt and disillusionment. 'I know now there are Americans who don't hate us,' he told me, 'and that makes a world of difference—just to have friends.' "

A Methodist minister who has been working among the Japanese in internment camps in Montana commented, "Your church is doing a fine job—but if it were in some other areas, it would be burned to the ground." He cited horror tales of hysteria such as we have feared, but have not found, in our area. It came over me suddenly, and with shock, that the soldiers who have been on guard have been here not to protect us from the Japanese so much as to protect the Japanese from us.

The evacuation was profitable to those who sought to exploit the troubled Japanese. Mr. Abe, whom we mentioned before, quotes from a memoir of one of his church members:

Yesterday two men came. They said they were our friends "trying to be helpful." They did not even take their hats off, and kept cigars in their mouths in the room. "We will pay a fair price for your household goods," they said. "Thirty dollars for the washing machine. Fifteen dollars for the piano. Twenty-five dollars for the furniture in the dining room. Twenty-five dollars for everything in the bedroom. Seventy dollars for the machine [automobile]."

It took us twenty years to accumulate all these. I just had paid for the washing machine. And the car was a 1940 Chevrolet, worth a thousand dollars at least. We were speechless. My wife was sobbing. And the men still puffed cigars, and looked at us scornfully.

"If you don't want to sell now, we won't press. Just phone me before you leave tomorrow morning, and we will come and give you the amount we have just offered."

I didn't know what to do for a moment. But my Japanese friends had told me that these people were in a gang and they had a set price to offer, so no matter who came, the price would have been the same. I had no one to move my furniture. There was no time to get enough help. They must have known that I was planning to sell anyway. So I said yes, and they gave me a few pieces of paper money. I held them in my hand. So this was all that all our thirty years' labor amounted to. One hundred and sixty-five dollars! And I hated the men with hats and cigars and their sneers.

I locked all doors. Inside, my wife and I packed what little we wanted to take with us. The children were asleep. There was, naturally, no time for us to sleep. I was too busy and too angry to sleep anyway. I was so angry that I was going to knock down the next white man who dared to come. About six o'clock in the morning, there was a knock on the front door. The pounding on the door was persistent and I got curious. I pulled the door just enough to ask, "Who are you?" I did not ask very nicely. Then came the shock and shame of my life.

The voice from the outside said, "We are from the Church Federation. Won't you let us help you carry your baggage? We have a car, so why don't you put your big pieces in it first? At the depot, the women of the churches have your breakfast ready. We thought since you are leaving so early, you would have no time to cook. So please feel free to help yourself when you get there."

What kindness! My heart was so moved, I let big tears fall—unlike a man. And I opened the door, humbled and grateful.

The churches up and down the coast served coffee, doughnuts, and sandwiches for the departing evacuees. They also prepared box luncheons. Church women helped mothers and children. All these were received with mixed feelings. The majority of the Japanese were grateful. Others felt that the churches' efforts were too little and too late. A few refused to take anything from the Caucasians.

On April 18, 1942, the Reverend Hideo Hashimoto, pastor of the Fresno Japanese Methodist Church, wrote to many of his personal friends throughout the country an inspired letter, which was reprinted in *Christianity and Crisis, Fellowship,* and other religious publications. It read:

On the eve of evacuation, I greet you with mixed feelings. The swift current of events following the outbreak of the present war has disrupted the lives of many of us. I must state at the outset that it has not all been unmixed evil. As a minister of Christ, I have gained valuable experience and opportunities of service that will strengthen and make more effective my ministry. But to the people whom I serve these months have been times of uncertainty, fear, and heartbreaking disappointments. Not that we have expected to lead normal lives, but it was a blow to America-loving, peaceful, permanent residents, to be suddenly classified as "enemy aliens" and receive treatment as such.

The impact has been an especially hard one for the Nisei, the American citizens of Japanese parentage. They have no home but this—no allegiance but the United States. Already over five thousand are in the U. S. Army. Suddenly they awoke on the morning of March 3, and discovered to their utter bewilderment that their own government has classified them as Class 3 "enemy aliens," ahead of German and Italian aliens.

As I go about busily engaged in welfare work among needy families; soliciting funds and food for welfare, understanding, and aid from Caucasian friends; helping with registrations, disposal and storage of real and personal property; finding renters for houses and businesses; collecting junk; trying to preach to the being-disillusioned on the meaning of the Cross; providing nursery and recreational facilities; and writing these letters and articles to widely scattered friends; being restricted to five miles and having to be in at 8:00 P.M., I cannot believe that only three and a half months ago I was traveling from one end of the continent to the other, attending the National Conference of Methodist Students at Urbana, Illinois, and visiting many of you.

In all these days, the heart-warming and encouraging experiences in the midst of darkness have been your thoughtful letters and the sympathy and help of the Caucasian friends who have helped us unstintedly. The real meaning of friendship and of the Christian fellowship that transcends the barriers of race and nations stands out in clear-cut relief in these heart-breaking days.

What the future holds for us is very uncertain, except for the definite knowledge that there will be untold suffering. But it is not the physical suffering that is the most difficult for us. We are willing to go a second mile in serving and suffering for our nation and for the principles for which she stands. But it is the feeling that we are men without a country, not by our choice but against our will by the decree of the Fourth Army.

However, when a feeling of being unjustly discriminated against is combined with physical hardship, it is next to unbearable. The induction centers, where three thousand to ten thousand people will be housed and fed, temporarily, have been built in about a week to ten days. There must be about fifteen or twenty of them, most of them in racetracks and county fairgrounds. Many of the durable buildings are made-over stables, but the majority of them are rough frame structures twenty feet by one hundred feet with small windows, tarpaper walls and roofs, and asphalt floors! About five families will be housed in each. Imagine a typical Japanese family of six or seven (not the average, because there are many newlyweds and single men and women) living in a single room twenty feet square, in these shacks during the typical Fresno summer weather of 105 degrees outside in the shade—perhaps 125 degrees inside (with asphalt floors!). No one knows where the people will be relocated from these centers. The Army has taken upon itself (or was forced by powerfully maneuvered minority "public" pressure) a task that is not its usual. The Army has done it as well as may be expected, but it is faced with almost insuperable difficulties.

I am to be evacuated and to enter into one of these concentration camps, for that is what they really are, with double barbed fences and all. I shall probably be responsible to between three thousand and five thousand souls in one of these, perhaps at Fresno Fairgrounds. Many old people will die. Many babies will be born and will die. (The largest group of Nisei is now in the early twenties.)   Many will pass away more because of the loss of all that they have worked for in their lifetime and the lack of something to live for.

I am to be their pastor, the minister of the gospel.   How am I to preach to them?   I do not ask in resentment or cynicism. There is nothing in my heart but the feeling of responsibility and the task to be done.   If I fail, who will undertake it?   I even feel that it is my providential opportunity to serve the people and the Master.   But more than ever before I feel humble in the face of the gigantic task.   I need your help and your prayers.

"It is better to light a candle than to curse the darkness." Let us all endeavor, in the name of our Master, to do our bit for his kingdom in these days of darkness.

The evacuation was carried out by the Army.   It was unprecedented, the largest enforced evacuation in the history of the nation.   However, order prevailed in all operations of evacuation.   No untoward incident was reported.

Congressman Tolan stated after the evacuation:

To many citizens of alien parentage in this country it has come as a profound shock that almost overnight thousands of persons have discovered that their citizenship no longer stands between them and the treatment accorded to any enemy alien within our borders in time of war . . .

The nation must decide and Congress must gravely consider, as a matter of national policy, the extent to which citizenship, in and of itself, is a guaranty of equal rights and privileges during time of war.   Unless a clarification is forthcoming, the evacuation of the Japanese population will serve as an incident sufficiently disturbing to lower seriously the morale of vast groups of foreign born among our people . . .

America is great because she has transcended the difficulties inherent in a situation which finds all races, all nationalities, all colors, and all creeds within her borders.   This breadth of vision must be applied to the present circumstances.

2

The Church in Exile

THE physical movement of the evacuees was placed under the supervision of the Wartime Civil Control Administration of the Army. Assembly centers were hastily constructed not far away from the centers of Japanese population. Parks, fairgrounds, and racetracks were used for those centers, with the wire fence and other equipment to make them camp-like enclosures. Charlotte and Royden Susu-Mago tell of their experiences with the church as they were moved into one of them, as follows:

When we arrived at the assembly center at Tulare Fair Grounds, which was to be our home for some three and a half months, we found that for two weeks the residents there had had no resident minister. In spite of lack of trained leadership, however, the active church people already had banded together in a church council, and services had been held each of the two Sundays, ministers from the neighborhood occupying the improvised pulpit. The Protestant Church Commission provided for the pulpit supply.

Finding that five thousand people had suddenly come to be imprisoned in their midst with, as they thought, no pastors among them, the Tulare Ministerial Association had appointed the Reverend Arthur Leslie Rice counselor at the camp. Several times he had gained admittance to confer with the new church council, asking what Christians outside could do to help, and what supplies they could furnish. When two Japanese ministers arrived, however, Mr. Rice felt that there no longer was need for him to come in, but offered to stand by with whatever services he and the Ministerial Association could offer. This attitude was greatly appreciated by both ministers and laymen, for there was a strong feeling that the religious growth that came out of this difficult situation could best be fostered by men who had been through the experience with the people.

A word should be said for the kind Christian folk who gave so many of their Sunday afternoons to lighten our imprisonment. Outsiders were not permitted in the camp, but we had a common meeting ground in the low-roofed, ceilingless, barracks "visiting room," with its picnic benches, its armed guards at the door, and its "all out at five o'clock." Occasionally people came all the way from Los Angeles or Riverside to visit friends. More often our visitors were Quakers or Brethren from the vicinity who had procured our names by one means or another and had asked for us at the gates. Two couples came faithfully almost every Sunday, bringing iced watermelon and iced tea, and ice-cold figs or peaches—rare treats on those afternoons of 110° in the shade! We would round up all the young people we could find and take them out for this second-hand breath of freedom.

The first Sunday after our arrival, a Sunday school was started on rickety wooden bleachers beside the race track. Worship services were held on the concrete grandstand. As the summer had already started and there was no shade, we soon found that to avoid wholesale heat prostration, it was necessary to hold both Sunday school and church services early in the mornings. Later we were permitted to use barracks schoolrooms for our church school. About four hundred children, young people, and young adults attended these classes. Church services were attended by about fifteen hundred. The Reverend Mr. Chapman and the Reverend Mr. Gillett, a former Congregational missionary in Kyoto, Japan, who had worked among the Japanese in Southern California prior to the war, were preachers at those services.

On one occasion, when the Buddhist group had invited the

Reverend Raymond Booth, a Quaker, to address their service, they approached us to ask whether we might not have a union Buddhist-Christian service. Our young people were enthusiastic over the idea, though their elders raised some objections. However, the service was held, having been carefully planned to include elements both groups could sincerely share, and inspired by the gracious words of Mr. Booth. That experience stands out as something we shall always remember of our days in the assembly center. The grandstand, holding 2,500 people, was full to the last seat, and latecomers stood about on the ground below.

The Japanese-speaking group were granted less freedom than the young people. Being still under Army supervision at that time, we were permitted no speeches or sermons in the Japanese language unless they were delivered by a Caucasian. Into this difficult situation the Japan missionaries stepped with a good will, and so it was possible to hold Japanese services also until this ban was lifted.

We wanted to erect a church, but these bare, barnlike structures were only the skeletons of churches. There remained the task of dragging scrap lumber several blocks in the hot sun from the scrap pile to the church sites, and of building platforms, benches, pulpits, lecterns, and altars, wooden candlesticks and crosses. The barracks had no inner walls or ceilings, and in the first church we made we set a spotlight behind the last rafter beam, which lighted the cross on the altar. The women of the church bought wine-red material for a curtain to hang behind the altar—and behold, a house of worship!

Now a "church" building was established, but the problem of finding an adequate teaching staff was staggering. The gap between the generations was so wide that there were few young church people of an age to teach classes. If there had not been the language difference, we could have used the older women of the church, but in the isolation of camp our children were already losing the best of their English and picking up Japanese expressions. Looking toward eventual return to the real America, when our children would attend church schools where English was spoken, we felt that it was vital that they be provided with the vocabulary of Christianity in their own native language—English. Fortunately, several of the center school teachers proved to be church people and helped out wonderfully.

A large number of college-age Nisei also proved to be of invaluable help to church programs in all camps. Outside workers who were given regular access to the centers for this purpose were able to render valuable advice and leadership, too.

The Reverend Everett W. Thompson went from Seattle to the assembly center called "Camp Harmony" in Washington. He wrote about that camp:

The Army made the rule that only three types of service would be held, Protestant, Catholic, and Buddhist, and asked the various denominations to cooperate to this end. This was known before people came to the camp, and committee meetings were held to work out plans. The pastors of our six Japanese churches arranged a rotation of speakers so that a service would be held in each fenced-off section of the camp (there were four separate sections), with a sermon in Japanese when that became permissible. In Seattle, the English services for the young people had never been provided by the Japanese pastors, but by Caucasian workers. The Council of Churches of Seattle asked me to serve as their representative in the camp to unify the program for the young people. There were some ten Caucasian workers from Seattle, three from Tacoma, and two from near-by Sumner who were interested in assisting regularly in the program. These had all been helping in the young people's work in the various churches before evacuation. Several of us were ordained and in the habit of leading our own denominational worship services. However, when the pastors from Seattle offered to come down and preach if this was desired, the young people in the camp were very eager to have them do so, and we regular workers devoted our attention to building up a federated Sunday school in each of the areas of the camp. Thus during the four months that the camp continued there, a constant stream of preachers from Seattle came down to speak, the young people themselves conducting the services and leading the choirs. We had brought hymnbooks and even pianos with us.

What the Seattle Council of Churches did through Mr. Thompson for Camp Harmony was typical of the services rendered by Councils of Churches in Portland and in northern and southern California, and by many other smaller councils and ministerial associations throughout the coast area.

We pause here a moment before following the evacuee into the relocation centers, and direct our thoughts, with the Reverend Hideo Hashimoto as our guide, upon the first three months "behind barbed wires."

Two opposing attitudes are developing in the psychology of the people. The first and the most obvious one is that of resentment and rebellion against the whole thing, which is now precipitating into a subconscious feeling of bitterness.

The second is that of cynicism, a "don't care" attitude, saying, "What's the use? Let's forget about the situation and enjoy this as much as we can." Many of us have both of these mixed in us. This is a natural consequence of a life like this. Nonetheless, it is dangerous to the health of our personalities.

We must first of all seek to be realistic and look at this whole thing, centering around the war, without flinching from the unpleasant facts. Secondly, we must remember that, in spite of the tragic situation confronting the world, there is a Power that is stronger than all the powers of evil. In the pitch darkness of a storm, the ship sails under the guidance of an unseen hand, which gives directions through the compass. So also, our Creator continues to control.

We ought to be constantly on guard lest we forget the injustice and the danger to our American democracy, informing the general public and cooperating with those who are trying to remedy the situation. At the same time, we should be endeavoring to live the cooperative community life in the centers with our sacrificial effort, and make this an opportunity for the practice of brotherhood.

Transfer from the assembly centers to ten more permanent relocation centers was merely a "change of guards." The President established the War Relocation Authority, an independent civilian agency, to administer the relocation centers, thus releasing the Army from the care of the evacuees.

But the establishment of relocation centers was not accomplished without understandable difficulty. Here again the churches did much to make the task of the government lighter.

Mr. Thompson reported again:

When in late August, 1942, the Minidoka relocation center was opened in south central Idaho, the vocal public opinion in Idaho was solidly opposed to this mass influx of a people hardly known to them but condemned by wild and false rumors of sabotage and spying. There were, moreover, unfavorable attitudes as a result of the fact that the Army had considered them too dangerous to be left on the coast, though everyone knew that Japanese invasion was now more and more improbable. This feeling was deepened by the fact that a large Boise construction firm had several hundred Idaho men working on Wake Island when it was taken by the Japanese. Many Idaho homes were among the very first to feel the heartache and heartbreak of war casualties. It was natural for them to assume that these people with Japanese names and faces were directly concerned with the death or imprisonment of these husbands and brothers of theirs. It was understood that the W.R.A. had gained the reluctant consent of the state authorities for this center only by promises that the great bulk of the people would be relocated outside the state of Idaho.

Early in the fall of 1942, a regular meeting of the Interdenominational Preachers' Meeting of the Snake River Valley (the whole general region in which the relocation center was located) invited me to attend and to tell them about the center, its people, and its Christian churches. Almost everything I had to say was strikingly new to them, but they were eager to replace current prejudices with facts and asked practically and earnestly, "What can we and our people do to help?" A variety of suggestions were made and within a few days there began a stream of good-will gifts to the camp that was to continue for months and years.

About a month later, the W.R.A. and the churches in the center cooperated to entertain the priests and pastors of all the neighboring churches, including Catholic, Protestant, and Buddhist, and lay representatives from all southern Idaho and even Salt Lake City. The day at the center gave visiting pastors and one layman from each church a chance to share in services conducted by Japanese pastors, mingle freely with Japanese church members at a big dinner given for the occasion, and visit in one or two homes, the visitors scattering over the center so that they went by twos and threes, not in a large sight-seeing crowd. Friendships resulted from that day that have lasted right down to the present. Personal correspondence was started and has increased with the passing months. The strangeness was gone. These were seen to be people like themselves with the same basic loyalties to God and to America. Also these visitors saw at first hand both the honest attempt of the government officials to provide decent living conditions and the serious handicaps to personality that any attempt to keep people behind barbed wire, in tar-paper barracks on the raw desert, and away from their fellow men, imposed.

Shortly there grew up a long series of invitations by which groups of church people from one near-by town after another came out to share in church services in Minidoka, or Hunt, as we came to call our desert city. And then the reverse invitations came and the government permitted them to be accepted —for a given group of our Japanese church people to go out for a few hours to attend a church service in a town ten to forty miles away. Soon many different churches had had one experience or the other, some both.

When at the approach of Christmas time an eighty-voice choir from the Minidoka center was ready to give a concert, the preachers' meetings in three near-by towns undertook to get other influential organizations in town to join with them in sponsoring the concerts, admission free, with an offering to aid the choir in the purchase of music. The choir was gowned and gave a polished performance to packed houses each time. And so the feeling grew that these were people, not "Japs" with all the reproach and contempt that that term carried; cultured people, not mere beet field labor. For the farms round about had needed help very badly with the harvest, and with much red tape it was arranged that some two thousand men and boys were to go out for the harvest season, living where they were employed, and free for that period to go into town for shopping, the movies, and church. But many thought of them as so much foreign labor and made no effort to get acquainted. And some who did were surprised to discover that one of their new farm hands was a college graduate, another owned a hotel in Portland, and a third had had forty men working on his own farm in Washington the previous summer. But if the beet harvest made a beginning at acquaintance, the concerts followed by receptions continued this process. When the choir gave a series of selections from the "Messiah" in the Minidoka center, visitors came from a number of towns around.

Through the winter and on into the spring and the following

summer, gifts of hymnbooks, Sunday school material, books for our Christian Worker's Library, cuttings and bulbs for Minidoka gardens continued to pour in.

District meetings of young people began to send regular invitations to our Minidoka church and almost without fail we were represented at all of them. In the state and district meetings of the various denominations, Minidoka young people and pastors were invited to take a part and did so. And when the summer assemblies were held in the Saw Tooth Mountains a hundred miles away, Minidoka was represented with a good-sized delegation. The assembly authorities were careful to make arrangements for a real intermingling so that there was no racial line drawn and everybody really felt at home, even those who had never seen a "Jap" before and had been somewhat startled by the prospect. Japanese and Caucasian young people slept in the same tents, ate at the same tables, worked together in discussion groups, committees, and dish-washing squads, and played together on the ball field and in the swimming pool.

How much the church came to mean to Christian leaders is told by an incident concerning a little girl. The Reverend Lester Suzuki wrote:

One evening, while we were sitting in a family circle, and such circles were rare, my oldest daughter began to ask, "Why can't we have our own bathroom, and our own kitchen, and our own house?" We said, "Well, we are supposed to go to the mess hall, to the community bathrooms, and to the community laundry, and so on, because everybody else does it."

Then she began to ask, "Why can't we go back to Los Angeles?" I looked at my wife and she looked at me, and I said, "Because Los Angeles is in the combat zone and it's dangerous to be there."

"How come Auntie Binny is not out of Los Angeles? She lives in Los Angeles." (Auntie Binny is a Caucasian missionary to Japan, who lived in Los Angeles and we visited her often.) That was a stunner, and we didn't know what to say, but I finally blurted out, "Well, Irene, the only reason Auntie Binny is not out of Los Angeles is because she is not of Japanese blood and your father and mother and grandfathers and grandmothers were Japanese." Then she asked, "Then why isn't Auntie Ginny in camp? She's a Japanese." (Auntie Ginny is my sister-in-law, living in Colorado). We said, "Well, Auntie Ginny lives in Colorado and Colorado people did not have to move out."

The whole conversation never satisfied her, but such was the thought of a very young American. The only answer that would be satisfactory to these young Americans would be for America to show and lead the way in building an American brotherhood where no one race would be discriminated against and pointed out for special treatment in time of war or peace, and the church, the church as a whole, is the only power that can consummate such a program.

The Reverend Sohei Kowta, a Presbyterian minister, appraised the church from still another angle:

The people who wanted to study the Bible, to attend services and meetings had far more freedom to do so than they had had before the evacuation. From that standpoint, center life was a great blessing to the Christian people. Naturally, the work of the churches in the centers was far more active than in the pre-evacuation days. This drew many Nisei who otherwise might have been outside the church today. The churches contributed much, in my opinion, to keep the morale of center life high.

Here let me insert a little episode that shows the power of the gospel in the life of its believers. In the early days in the center, the people were bitter and nothing satisfied them. They spent their time in complaining. One day, a Japanese woman sat with my family in the mess hall and took lunch

4

with us. She was a total stranger to us. We talked casually about different things with her. After the lunch was over, I returned to my room with my wife, to whom I said, "I think that woman has some kind of religion. Maybe she is a Christian." My wife asked, "What makes you think so?" "She talked so differently from the rest of the people here." "What do you mean?" she asked again. "Well, didn't you notice?" I asked. "She used a certain expression twice while we were talking—an expression so unusual—an expression so rarely heard in the center. She said, '*Kansha-desuné*' [I am thankful] twice. I think she is a Christian. I will find out." I found out on the following day that she was a Christian woman! The Christians in the relocation center learned the truth that was uttered by St. Paul many centuries ago, "To them that love the Lord all things work together for good!"

The Susu-Magos, moved to Arizona, found Christians ready and willing to help. They reported:

Our contacts with the outside were mostly through letters. However, we were fortunate in having a returned Congregational missionary, the Reverend William McKnight, stationed in Phoenix, and a former Methodist missionary in Japan, the Reverend S. A. Stewart, who had a small Japanese church in Mesa. These two men came into our camp, offering to do anything that needed doing. What could they buy for us in Phoenix or Mesa? Once again we were deeply grateful for their tact and helpfulness. They ran a regular "shopping service," searching Phoenix and Mesa and other towns for scarce articles for the needs of the people, getting up early in the morning to search the want ads for coolers, baby carriages, and other nonbuyables, and racing off at seven o'clock in the morning to procure these scarcities for someone in camp.

This, however, was only part of the service they rendered us—the whole of which we shall probably never know. They preached for us in one and then another of the chapels. Mr.

McKnight taught a class of young people. They used their cars to bring in church groups from outlying towns, or take out a group from camp to meet with some church or attend a conference. Such social contacts as these might have been more numerous but for the attitude of the people of Arizona, led by the organized farming industry. The governor periodically deferred to these opposition groups by refusing to grant leave for people from camp to visit any town in Arizona. This had a very serious effect on camp morale.

Mr. McKnight and Mr. Stewart did us excellent service throughout the state by addressing groups, urging that the governor be more democratic. Their visits to camp were always cause for rejoicing, and I think they did more than anyone else to keep us feeling a part of the world outside.

Keeping the evacuee a part of the world "outside" was indeed one of the most valuable things the Christian groups and organizations did. The Susu-Magos wrote further:

Occasionally we were asked to send delegations of young people to summer camps. After a year and more of isolation from American life, the sense of being free, even for a week's time, and the association with normal American young people were experiences that meant much to the lucky delegates. They came back to camp like a fresh breeze blowing, and made breathing just a little easier for their friends. One of the most rewarding elements of these summer camp visits was the feeling, which several expressed on their return, that they had been able to create in the Caucasian delegates a better understanding of the Nisei and their problems. They all seemed to meet with widespread misunderstanding of the evacuation program. One of our girls reported a delegate saying to her, "Do you mean to say they put you, an American citizen, into a concentration camp?" "Yes, me and seventy thousand other American citizens," replied our delegate.

Miss Beatrice Elizabeth Allen, on the staff of the Girls'

Friendly Society of the Protestant Episcopal Church, stated that seven or eight girls in the junior and younger member groups corresponded regularly with girls in Rivers, Arizona. Some of them exchanged gifts and pictures.

It is interesting to note that one of these Japanese American girls, Miss Grace Nakada, had six brothers in the service of our country, one of whom has been awarded the Purple Heart. One of the juniors remarked, "I don't see why they have to be called *Japanese* Americans, when their letters show them to be patriotic American citizens the same as we are."

From one camp came this reaction:

I have become reconciled here—but those first two weeks! How I suffered mentally! I hated being kept here. I kept thinking of some great wrong I had done to be punished in such a manner, but I could think of nothing to merit this. . . . I couldn't understand why I was different from any of you, born and bred in California with no other home to claim; raised on hot dogs and baseball just as all Americans are; as proud of the Stars and Stripes and the Constitution as each and every American should be. . . . To have all that suddenly taken away from me—the more I thought about it, the more confused I became!

You don't know what part you played in my life when you sent the Girls' Friendly Society program "United We Make America." I was feeling rather discouraged about a few things pertinent to the situation of the Japanese Americans when your material came. It made me feel so good to have that material and the program presented in it. It makes me doubly glad that I belong to the G.F.S.

It was not Christian organizations alone that tried to give the residents in the centers a sense of unity with the outside world. The Red Cross, P.T.A., Camp Fire Girls, Boy Scouts, and various intercultural, interracial, and international organizations also maintained excellent contacts.

Let us now turn our attention to the two national Christian associations that contributed to the morale of the evacuees. Mr. Masao Satow of the Y.M.C.A. says that during the time of the evacuation Y.M.C.A. secretaries on the West Coast rendered personal services to the people who had to evacuate; and though the Y.M.C.A. was barred from the assembly centers, in the fall of 1942, Mr. George Corwin, Senior Secretary for Boys' Work, visited a number of the relocation centers and encouraged the formation of the Y.M.C.A. in some of them. The Y.M.C.A. in Manzanar started under this stimulus, and in the spring of 1943, a number of Y.M.C.A. secretaries and laymen from Los Angeles visited at Manzanar and took equipment with them for the Manzanar Y.M.C.A.

The West Central Area Council of the Y.M.C.A. sent a representative to Heart Mountain and this was the beginning of the Heart Mountain Y.M.C.A. Rocky Mountain student Y.M.C.A. secretaries were responsible for getting things started at Granada. Both Granada and Heart Mountain sent representatives to the Area Council meetings in 1943 and 1944. The Pueblo Association asked the West Central Area Council for permission to welcome officially the Granada Y.M.C.A. into the Council fellowship, so in April of 1943, twelve board members and secretaries visited Granada and joined in a joint meeting and worship service with the Granada Y.M.C.A. members.

A Hi-Y club was formed at Minidoka and Tule Lake through the visits of Y.M.C.A. secretaries.

The St. Louis Association "adopted" the two relocation centers in Arkansas and secretaries made visits to Rohwer and Jerome.

The National Council of the Y.M.C.A. made funds available for definite services to the relocation centers in the spring of 1943 of a full-time staff person, equipment, attendance at conferences and meetings, and the employment of "Y" coordinators in the centers. Mr. Masao Satow was the staff person employed.

Later, the Pacific Southwest Area Council added to its staff Mr. Dwight Welch, to work among youth in the centers in the Pacific Southwest Area.

Miss Esther Briesmeister of the Y.W.C.A. reported that the first Y.W.C.A. in a relocation center was started at Manzanar, in August of 1942. One of the national leaders, who had been out on the West Coast during the five-month period of the evacuation, stayed long enough to fulfill her promise that there would be a Y.W.C.A. if people wanted it.

During the following three years, the Association organized a program in each of the ten relocation centers, under the direction of an advisory committee of twelve or fifteen women and with one person acting as the Y.W.C.A. secretary at each camp. In every center, the program was organized and carried out by former staff members, board women, club members, and students who had been a part of the local associations on the West Coast. Many of these volunteers were exceedingly able and intelligent leaders, and they tackled jobs that would have challenged even the most astute professional worker. The work continued for two and a half years and, even though these women were constantly relocating, there were others who stepped to the front and took their share of responsibility for keeping the organization going. The enthusiasm for the Y.W.C.A. was expressed in the words of one of the mothers, who said that "the Girl Reserves started meeting before they had their suitcases unpacked!"

Young adult women started their clubs again and the young matrons began meeting to make plans for themselves and for their small children. The college students and their contemporaries began to organize "college bound" clubs, trying to keep alive an interest in higher education. The older Issei women in some of the centers formed groups of their own and had informal meetings to discuss some of their problems. Often they discussed how they could help the younger people to build the Y.W.C.A. Interesting discussions were held in the early days in the relocation centers, on the question, "What can an organization like the Y.W.C.A. do in a community like this?" The Y.W.C.A. found that its contributions might be made in a variety of ways. It works with all people regardless of race, creed, color, religion, or social or economic background.

Therefore, the Y.W.C.A. was the logical organization to cut across some of the differences in the community and to begin the building of better relationships between the various groups. While there was no variety in the racial pattern, there were religious differences, which tended to create problems as people tried to live in such compact communities. The Association helped people to have a sense of personal adequacy, through exploring and acquiring new skills as individuals, and through the organization of clubs that offered opportunities for young people to assume leadership and to be important in the eyes of their own group. It was also able, at various times, to provide outside leadership to help in the development of the program in the camps.

In these ways, the people in the relocation centers realized that they were still part of a national and international organization. This realization was made vivid through the neighborliness of local Associations near the centers. Conferences were planned in the relocation centers, as well as in the local communities, with a two-way flow of leadership going out of the center to the local communities, and Y.W.C.A. members from the outside coming in.

The philosophy upon which the Y.W.C.A. operates— that the qualities common to all human beings regardless of race, creed, or color, far exceed the differences that divide them—has stood up under the severe test of these past few years. What the Y.W.C.A. has meant to the people in the centers has been well expressed by one of the Nisei workers:

For our members in the centers, the actions of the Y.W.C.A.'s all over the nation have meant many and lovely things : continued faith in some ideas in the midst of shaken beliefs ; the encouraging help of friends through the Associations in out-of-the-way places that had until now been mere names of places ; the full realization of the size of the organization and the knowledge that, in the evacuees' plans for a new life, they could look with confidence toward someone. In all the difficulties they faced, they knew that, somewhere, there were other women intensely interested and concerned. For the first time, it gave many a deeper and closer understanding of other people who have faced difficulties and injustices in many ways more poignant than theirs, and it gave them a warm sympathy that had been but academic before.

America's Biggest Christmas Party *

As the holiday season approached in 1942, people in different parts of the country began to wonder what Christmas was going to mean to the little Americans with Japanese faces living in ten relocation centers.

Just who had the inspiration in the first place was lost sight of in the general excitement, but the suggestion of providing Christmas gifts for children in the relocation centers was taken up with enthusiasm by one group after another. The initiative in organizing the plan was taken by the Home Missions Council. A hurry call was sent to women's units of home mission boards of the various denominations and they at once enlisted the membership of their local churches. Others were delighted to help. The Japanese American Citizens League secured essential lists and addresses in Washington, and worked tirelessly for the success of the venture; the American Friends Service Committee had already sent a letter to Sunday schools of its membership; the Fellowship of Reconciliation gave publicity to the plan; the magazine *Common Ground* circularized its list of subscribers; Japanese American churches on the "outside" participated, and Y.W.C.A. groups of Girl Reserves shared in the project.

Though it was November before the bright idea began to materialize and nearly all the denominations and other groups had made their Christmas plans, the outpouring of gifts was nothing short of astounding—many giving far beyond their quotas of presents for the children and some

* "The Story of America's Biggest Christmas Party" is reprinted here, by permission, from a leaflet of the Home Missions Council.

sending generous gifts of cash in addition, so that there would be Christmas trees, treats for adults as well as children, and delicacies for patients in the center hospitals.

Winter came unexpectedly to the people of the relocation center. Dislocated, without their own homes for the second time within a year, the people had begun again to make homes out of their bare rooms in the centers. While the men hammered and sawed pieces of furniture out of scrap lumber, the women were busy with needle and thread. A palmetto branch stuck in a glass fruit jar, a colorful spray of autumn leaves breaking the bleakness of the raw-lumber walls, a few pictures of their old home—and a new home was born.

Then, suddenly, a voice overheard amid the chatter while waiting in the dining hall line, "Say, next week is Christmas!" A feeling of despair filled the mothers. Christmas but a week off! "What are we going to do for our children?" But throughout the nation, friends had not forgotten. On Christmas, Santa Claus, through these friends, came to the children of the centers—he had not failed them even in a world filled with strange and sudden changes.

A woman living in one of the centers wrote an account of the Christmas celebration there:

We set up Santa's Workshop, and, as box after box came in and the contents were displayed, it was a wonderful sight to see. When the final count was taken, there were 17,000 gifts from more than 860 persons and organizations located in practically every state in the Union. Those who helped in the distribution of gifts were amazed at the fact that there were total strangers, as well as friends, who had love and concern for persons of Japanese ancestry in such times as these.

A shining cross and a slowly rising moon formed the setting for a festival of sacred music beautifully described in one camp newspaper:

From the opening strains of "O Come, All Ye Faithful" as the choir of two hundred marched single-file over the embankment, not unlike over the hills of Judea, to the final Amen of Mallote's "The Lord's Prayer," the appreciative audience of approximately one thousand was richly and deeply entranced. The opening anthem was sung in Latin. Schubert's "The Lord Is My Shephard" was sung to sheer perfection from its softest pianissimo to the loudest fortissimo.

The following is from a letter from another camp:

We wish you could have been at our Christmas worship program on the Sunday before Christmas. Over eighty-five young men and women of the mass choir came down the aisle in their robes singing, "O Come, All Ye Faithful." They sat in front of an improvised altar, beautiful because of a cross that hung between the folds of a draped velvet background. On the piano was a tumbleweed, potted in a crêpe-paper-covered tin can. It was decorated with red stars. As we heard the familiar Scripture reading of the first Christmas and the lovely strains by the choir from Handel's "Messiah," our faith in the Prince of Peace was strengthened.

One heart-warming surprise was the participation in the Christmas giving by groups of various racial backgrounds. Outstanding in the reports is the mention of Chinese groups. A letter from a national missionary society says, "We have a Chinese Christian center in California. That little center took up our challenge and immediately collected gifts for their Japanese friends." The same letter continues, "In Philadelphia, we have an Italian center. The appeal was made to all departments of the Sunday school. Three Sundays they brought in their money. One boy had eleven pennies, usually spent on candy during school recess. Those pennies with many others helped to send twenty-five dollars to be used for the Japanese."

In some cases the true spirit of Christmas was revealed in letters sent to the camps with the gifts. In an article headed "Christmas Gifts Come from All over America," appearing in a camp paper, this fact was stressed:

Letters accompanying packages and checks or money orders often revealed the thought and sacrifice behind many of the gifts. Some were hand made—crocheted yarn dolls were made by Spanish-American boys in New Mexico. Also from New Mexico a box was sent by the eight pupils enrolled in the mission school high up in the mountains. The teachers co-operated in obtaining articles from a dime store forty miles away, and their own little store was set up at the school. Some children brought pumpkins, wheat, chickens, and other farm products to exchange for little gifts.

The largest single gift at one center came from four thousand students of a high school in Honolulu—a check for five hundred dollars with the suggestion that it be spent for athletic equipment for the three camp high schools. Another center was surprised by a gift from a group of American soldiers who heard of the party and chipped in a dollar each. There were seventy-four who contributed, most of them Nisei, but some of them Caucasian brothers-in-arms and one a Chinese American. Trimmings for the Christmas trees in a third camp were donated by a store in a different state through the influence of a minister in yet another state!

Many of the government representatives, chiefs of community service, and directors of relocation centers sent words of appreciation. One said, "We feel that expressions of interest as typified by the Christmas gifts sent to us is an assurance that democracy and good will are still characteristics of our great country. Could those outside the center have witnessed the many expressions of appreciation and gratitude for the remembrances at Christmas time, we are sure that they would be fully repaid for their efforts in behalf of the residents of the center." A chief of the Community Management Division wrote, "I take off my hat to the Protestant churches."

In reading the letters and newspaper articles from the relocation centers, one is deeply impressed with the fact that these fellow Americans of ours and many who would have become Americans if our country had welcomed them, saw something much more than a "Merry Christmas" in this unexpected demonstration of friendship. A few sentences will indicate the spirit that permeated the messages:

Seeing all these gifts coming in from religious groups has made me think more seriously of spiritual matters than I've ever done before. . . . Never before was "Joy to the World" sung with such profound meaning and never was the real message of Christmas so keenly felt. . . . Before the gifts were distributed by the Boy Scouts we had a dedication service of the gifts, expressing gratitude to all the donors and explaining the meaning of Christmas to all. . . . And to the parents of the center, peace and serenity descended once more on the day of birth of the Prince of Peace. Peace was a word fraught with meaning—peace in their hearts at the thought of good friends, "peace on earth," their prayer. "Good will to men" shown to these people by men of good will and women and children on the outside brought tears to these people, tears that come from a full heart. We shall always remember this event as a light in the darkness of this war. . . . "We are deeply impressed and humbly grateful for your share in this expression of Christian brotherliness. We know that the spirit of Christ lives on despite hatred and strife.

The letter from which the last quotation came was signed not only by the representatives of the Protestant churches, the Women's Federation, and the Community Council of the center, but by the minister of the Buddhist church. In another letter was this significant sentence, "As one non-churchman said, 'The church is the only one you can depend upon today,' so it was and we are very grateful for the church and our part of making the church more useful for God."

3

The Church Prepares for Relocation

THE detention in relocation centers of seventy thousand citizens rested heavily upon the conscience of government officials and other citizens who were mindful of the ideals of American democracy. The first year of the relocation centers was marked by discussions, resolutions, and other actions of bodies feeling concern all over America. Particularly restless was the Christian church. American Protestantism seldom speaks or acts as one body. But upon the problem of the Japanese Americans, the churches agreed spontaneously and unanimously. Conservatives and liberals, pacifists and non-pacifists, all felt the same. The *Christian Century* and *Christianity and Crisis* agreed! The *Christian Century* was most persistent in its expressed concern for Japanese Americans. In almost every issue of this Christian weekly was to be found at least one reference to the plight of the evacuees. Numerous denominational magazines also carried news and articles on the evacuation. All deplored the relocation centers and demanded quick government action to restore citizenship rights to loyal citizens.

As early as April 29, 1942, the following letter was addressed to the President of the United States by church representatives:

Many leaders of the Protestant churches are expressing their concern about our national policy with respect to United States citizens of Japanese parentage, which jeopardizes our democracy and has a bearing on religious liberty. . . .

One feature of the present regulations gives us especially grave concern. American citizens of Japanese parentage, but born and raised in this country, are being uprooted from their homes and normal occupations without hearings or any other process of classification whereby the loyal are distinguished from those of proved or supposed disloyalty. . . . Such abrogation of the rights of citizens is especially unfortunate in view of the fact that, since the measures are not being applied in the same way to citizens of German and Italian lineage, the Japanese conclude that we are practising race discrimination.

. . . Here in the United States we have an uneasy conscience because this policy savors of totalitarianism and discrimination. . . . Abroad, reports of our policy will undoubtedly be exploited to arouse distrust of the sincerity of our democratic professions and thus undermine America's prestige and influence.

> *Signed:* LUTHER A. WEIGLE, *President*
> Federal Council of the Churches
> of Christ in America
>
> G. PITT BEERS, *President*
> Home Missions Council of
> North America
>
> ALMON R. PEPPER, *Chairman*
> Commission on Aliens and
> Prisoners of War

The following resolution of the Presbyterian Church in the U.S.A., passed at the General Assembly in June, 1942, is quoted as a typical expression of the concern of the various denominations:

We are deeply grieved at the situation forced upon American citizens of Japanese parentage and upon those Japanese who are aliens only because our laws forbade them citizenship.

The enforced segregation of American citizens of whatever nationality or race, although convicted of no wrong, has dangerous possibilities and necessitates a serious consideration of our present and future policy. . . . We urge that serious study be given now to the problem of the resettlement of the Japanese and their re-establishment in the normal life of the community. . . . We believe that the announcement of a fair policy in this respect now will strengthen the cause of democracy with the millions of the colored races the world over. . . . Deeply concerned at the enforced impairment of civil liberties involved in this situation and others, we urge upon our legislators, our public authorities and voluntary groups, that our institutions of freedom be jealousy guarded and respected, even in proved military necessity.

On its part, too, the government was gravely concerned with the future of the people, especially the American citizens, in the relocation centers. The conditions within the camps were not conducive to a proper up-bringing of Americans. While all competent observers of the camps agreed that the management of the War Relocation Authority was humane and fair, the concentration of a people of one racial background could not be considered American. Furthermore, the enforced mode of living—rooms in barracks, meals in mess halls, uniform nominal wage schedules (twelve, sixteen, or nineteen dollars per month depending on skill or its lack)—tended to break down the morale of the evacuees. Especially tragic was the degeneration of unit family life under the impact of the concentrated institutional life.

Besides, as long as the Japanese people were in the relocation centers, they remained easy targets of attack for a hysterical press and bigoted individuals. (Some of the most

5

vicious attacks upon them were made by a section of our press in the very first months of the relocation centers.)

Raising the question of the loyalty of Japanese Americans became a favorite source of discussion by those who tried to discredit both the War Relocation Authority and the evacuees. Most widely used was the rumor that Japanese Americans had engaged in sabotage and other Fifth Column activities at the time of the Pearl Harbor attack. Since 1942 was an election year, the "Japanese problem" in California provided particularly profitable ammunition for race-mongering politicians. One of them told his constituents that Japanese Americans had "proved to be treacherous and untrustworthy as a race." * Dishonesty, deceit, and hypocrisy were named as innate racial characteristics of the Nisei.

To the charges of sabotage, categorical denials were made; *e.g.,* Assistant Attorney General Rowe said on April 20, 1942, "Mr. John Edgar Hoover, director of the Federal Bureau of Investigation, has informed me that there was no sabotage committed there [in Hawaii] prior to December 7, on December 7, or subsequent to that time."

The fact of the loyalty of the Nisei as a group has since been definitely established by the acts of the Nisei themselves. We need at this point, however, to remind ourselves that until this question was settled in the minds of the public, the War Relocation Authority labored under a heavy and most embarrassing handicap.

The officials of the W.R.A., including the first director, Mr. Milton S. Eisenhower (brother of the general), and Mr. Dillon S. Myer, his successor, both of whom had come

---

* Quoted in *Outcasts,* by Caleb Foote, p. 12. New York, Fellowship of Reconciliation.

from the Department of Agriculture, and the staff members, deserve the churches' hearty commendation for their wise handling of the difficult situation. On their part, the churches stood by the W.R.A. and the evacuees against groundless attacks from irresponsible sources.

The W.R.A. was convinced that the relocation center system was un-American—a conviction shared by many visitors—and that the only solution was the release of the people. Yet, without an assurance that released evacuees would be favorably received by outside communities, it could do nothing except "hold" them as long as necessary.

The first break in this deadlock came in the summer of 1942. Sugar beet growers in areas near certain centers, faced with acute manpower shortage, asked the W.R.A. if the evacuees could be released to harvest the crop. The authorities were interested and the evacuees were willing and anxious to go.

The direct result of this experiment was the saving of valuable sugar, enough to supply the rationed portions of ten million Americans that year. But the by-products were equally valuable. Several thousand evacuees went back to the centers not only with money but with confidence in themselves. They had demonstrated once and for all that when people worked and lived with them, prejudices changed into acceptance. This had been proved earlier by the visits of church groups, but those church contacts were necessarily temporary and under favorable circumstances. The sugar beet harvesting now proved that the *general* public was sufficiently tolerant to let the evacuees earn a living.

Encouraged by this experience, the W.R.A. began consultations with the War Department and the Department of

Justice, with a view to setting up a large-scale dispersal relocation program.

Others also were thinking. On September 24, 1942, a strategic conference was held in New York. Representatives of the Federal Council of Churches, the Home Missions Council, the Foreign Missions Conference, the various denominations, the W.R.A., and the Japanese American Citizens League were present.

A report was made that the churches, aware of the difficult position of the Japanese Americans before the war, had organized an Inter-Council Committee on Japanese Work, with a view towards educating the church constituents regarding it. After Pearl Harbor, the Commission on Aliens and Prisoners of War was established to handle problems in that field. The plight of the evacuees was in one sense a matter of concern to that commission because the evacuees were virtual prisoners. Yet it was reluctant to administer work for them, because the majority of the evacuees were American citizens, and they were not prisoners of war.

An independent agency to promote the resettlement of Japanese Americans was imperative.

At this point, Mr. Thomas Holland and Mr. John Provinse of the W.R.A. presented the government's plan for resettlement. According to their statement, the evacuee could now apply for "leave clearance." The application would be studied at the relocation center and together with all available data on the applicant sent to the Washington headquarters of the W.R.A. for further study and final judgment. In Washington, the applicant's record would be checked against the records of intelligence agencies, and if it was found sufficiently reasonable that the release of a person would not jeopardize the interests of the country, "clearance" would be authorized.

At the relocation center, the applicant was to be required to show that he had assurance of employment and a place to live. The W.R.A. would obtain reasonable assurance that the coming of an evacuee to a community outside of the military areas would not disturb order and security there, and would open offices in several key cities in the Midwest to handle matters relative to resettlement.

On October 1, the W.R.A. made public the procedures for resettlement, with the appropal of the War Department, the Department of Justice, and the War Manpower Commission.

On October 7, 1942, another meeting of the church representatives was held in New York and it was decided to set up a committee to administer the churches' work on resettlement. As a result of this meeting there was formed the Committee on Resettlement of Japanese Americans, sponsored jointly by the Federal Council of Churches and the Home Missions Council, in cooperation with the Foreign Missions Conference. On its executive committee were Dr. Hermann N. Morse, chairman, Dr. Roswell P. Barnes, Dr. Mark A. Dawber, Dr. John W. Thomas, and Dr. J. Quinter Miller, secretary-treasurer. Mr. George E. Rundquist, a Quaker business man who had given up his publishing work and who was serving voluntarily for Japanese Americans in connection with the New York Church Committee for Japanese Work, was invited to become executive secretary of the Committee on Resettlement of Japanese Americans.

Soon after his appointment Mr. Rundquist went to Chicago, where, on October 25, another important meeting was called by the W.R.A. Again representatives of the churches, the Y.M.C.A., the Y.W.C.A., and other agencies were present, and resettlement possibilities were discussed.

In order to make resettlement possible, a favorable community sentiment was essential. It was also necessary to find employers and places for resettlers to live. In 1942, when the war hung in the balance, this seemed an extremely difficult task. But as those present expressed their views, representing wide ranges of community life, resettlement came to seem not only possible but highly desirable. For it would relieve, though only in small measure it was true, the existing acute manpower shortage. Also, it was in accordance with the professed principles of the United States.

In Chicago, there already existed the Chicago Advisory Committee for Evacuees, sponsored by the American Friends Service Committee, which had been rendering service to voluntary evacuees. This committee assumed responsibility for Chicago.

Mr. Rundquist proceeded to other cities and assisted in organizing local resettlement committees. Before long the following cities had both Citizens' Resettlement Committees and W.R.A. offices functioning: Chicago, Minneapolis, St. Paul, Madison (Wisconsin), Milwaukee, Cleveland, Peoria, Detroit, St. Louis, Kansas City (Missouri), and Indianapolis. In all these committees, while every effort was made to secure the widest possible cooperation of citizen leaders and representation, the nucleus of members came from the local Council of Churches and other Christian groups.

The Committee on Resettlement published two pamphlets to help explain resettlement procedure and the background of the evacuees. It also started a monthly information sheet called *Resettlement Bulletin*. This proved immensely popular. Within six months the circulation grew from the first issue of 500 to 2,500.

Local committees swung into action, and opportunities for employment were explored. Friends of the evacuees rallied around the W.R.A. to strengthen its program of resettlement. The "outside" was getting ready, though slowly.

Inside the centers, those wishing to return to freedom applied for "leave clearance." Procedures adopted for this clearance were necessarily complicated, requiring much time and red tape.

Personal friends who lived outside the prohibited area of the West Coast wrote to the W.R.A. asking (and demanding) that the release of their evacuee friends be facilitated. Individual ministers and church organizations also offered employment and living quarters. Their anxiety to have the evacuees come out was matched by the similar desire of the evacuees to go out. But those procedures! They took so long. There was restlessness in many churches and organizations during the winter of 1942.

4

From the Church in the Center
to the Church Outside

THE movement of the people from the camps into outside communities began in earnest in the spring of
1943. It is significant that most of those who first came out
were members of the relocation center churches.

What the various Christian organizations had done
through the period of the assembly centers and the first few
months in the relocation centers to make the people feel
they were a part of the world was perhaps the most potent
factor in building the confidence of the Christian evacuees.
Equally important was the living power of Christianity to
revitalize waning interest in active life. Without realizing
it, many evacuees were becoming complacent and even cyn-
ical about everything.

The churches did a number of things the year around to
keep alive the evacuees' hope and interest in life. Since the
official agency of the church to work among the center residents was the Protestant Church Commission for Japanese Service, that commission supplied most of the equipment for the center churches: hymnals, Bibles, Sunday
school materials, chairs, pianos. All these were either trans-
ported from the former Japanese churches or donated by
the West Coast churches through the Commission. Without them, the church activities in the centers would not

have been so nearly normal as they were. And without this normalcy of the centers' religious activities, it is doubtful if the people would have been ready to make the transition from camp to normal life with as much confidence as they showed.

Another contribution of the Commission was the supplying of religious workers, who were, most of the time, the only non-Japanese at the centers with the exception of government officials. How essential this provision was to the overcoming of fear cannot be measured unless one has lived the life of segregation in camp. As has already been noted, the church sent in a constant stream of creative visitors. Besides the members of the Commission who entered the relocation centers regularly to conduct religious services, near-by ministers and church people, and representatives of denominational and interdenominational headquarters assisted the center churches. That these visitors came in a steady stream, unlike curious reporters or investigation officials from Washington, gave proof that they were sincerely interested in the welfare of the people. When the evacuees went out, they could call upon these friends. This also gave them confidence and courage.

The highlight of these activities was the Christian mission sponsored by the Department of Evangelism of the Federal Council of Churches. The Reverend Hideo Hashimoto wrote from the Jerome relocation center in Arkansas, on May 31, 1943, of what the mission accomplished:

We [have] just concluded the most blessed six days of the Christian mission, held in this center, May 16-21. It was a rather new experience for all of us, including Dr. Jesse M. Bader, the originator of the National Christian Mission. The

Federal Council is planning to hold these missions in each of the relocation centers this year. I certainly encourage each center to undertake it. The team here consisted of Dr. Albert P. Shirkey, of the Travis Park Methodist Church, San Antonio, Texas, the mass meeting speaker and leader of the seminar on "Being Christian in Time of Conflict"; Mrs. Jesse B. Eubank, leader of the seminar on "Marriage and the Home"; the Reverend John B. Cobb, of the Spokane Japanese Methodist Church, Japanese mass meeting speaker and seminar leader on "Spiritual Growth"; and Miss Jesse M. Trout, former secretary to Doctor Kagawa of Japan, leader of the seminar on "The Bible and the Home" (in Japanese). Besides these full-time members, we had Dr. E. Stanley Jones on Thursday evening and Friday morning; Dr. Harold W. Tribble of the Southern Baptist Theological Seminary, Louisville, Kentucky, at the Friday evening mass meeting; and Dr. Jesse M. Bader. We had from two hundred to three hundred and fifty attending each of the two (English and Japanese) mass meetings every night and about eleven hundred Thursday evening. More than two hundred rededicated their lives to Christ in the English mass meetings alone. Some thirty accepted Jesus Christ for the first time, and nine were baptized during the mission week. It was a wonderful experience for all of us.

It is pleasant to have a minister in a relocation center appraise the work of the church like this. But lest we lose sight of the background against which the mission was conducted, let us learn more from the same source. Mr. Hashimoto's analysis of the situation is in agreement with what most Christian leaders felt at that time:

May 15 marked the anniversary of my entry into the Fresno assembly center. These last twelve months [have] provided me with rich, unexpected opportunities for service and experience, as well as heartaches in seeing the trampling down of civil liberties and a great deal of suffering on the part of the Japanese

Americans. There have been some excellent articles on the evacuation, many of them understanding and fair. I need not repeat
what they have said of the heat, dust, food, prison psychology
of administration, and the humiliation of it all at the assembly
center, or the deadening and stagnating life in the relocation
center. I find the W.R.A. personnel and policy to be well-
meaning and progressive, though not always efficient or wise
in carrying out the policies. The present W.R.A. plan of dispersal resettlement is a constructive and forward-looking one.
However we should not lose sight of the whole injustice of the
evacuation especially for the American citizens who comprise
two-thirds of the total evacuated population.

In all the different phases of the evacuation, a blot on our
democracy, the basic issue is that of civil liberties—not so much
what the American citizens of Japanese ancestry had to go
through, for many in the nation and in the world are endur-
ing immeasurably greater suffering, but the way in which our
Bill of Rights suffered a fundamental setback at the hands of
small, organized, prejudiced minorities. This is already prov-
ing to be an embarrassment for the United Nations and an
Axis weapon in the ideological and political phases of the war.
Many progressive and Christian leaders are working for the
reversal of the policy. The outburst of Lieutenant General
John L. DeWitt of the Western Defense Command, "A Jap's a
Jap," is a direct result of a move of this sort. The war for
freedom as well as the defense of our national integrity and
tradition make it imperative that the evacuation order be
rescinded. "Eternal vigilance is the price of liberty."—Thomas
Jefferson.

If, as we have indicated, the Christian churches and ministers in the centers were the chief instrumentation in sending their people out, church pastors and people on the outside were chiefly responsible for making the resettlement
as easy as possible.

Wherever the evacuees have gone groups of Christians

have played an important rôle in the relocation program.
In St. Louis the Congregational Christian Church had a
service committee. In Washington, D. C., it was the well
informed leadership of church people that encouraged other
groups to help prepare for the coming of evacuees. In
Philadelphia and Boston, citizens' committees were organized with Christian laymen as chairmen. In New York
City, the New York Church Committee for Japanese Work
had been set up by the boards of domestic missions of interested denominations immediately after Pearl Harbor, to
minister to some two thousand resident Issei and Nisei, and
later to incoming evacuees. It expanded its membership and
slightly changed its name when the challenge to assist resettlers came, and included them also in its program.

Among the church-related organizations, the Y.M.C.A.'s
and Y.W.C.A.'s stand out both at the national and local
levels. They not only opened their dormitory facilities, but
served actively as employment agencies. Services rendered
by non-church organizations, whose members, nevertheless,
were motivated by the sense of Christian fellowship, also
are worthy of note. Among them, the Women's International League for Peace and Freedom and the Fellowship of
Reconciliation were most active. The League had a Japanese American Resettlement Committee and participated in
sponsoring a hostel in Philadelphia. The F.O.R. established
a resettlement loan fund.

One F.O.R. member, a woman in Denver, learned that
when a Nisei family leased a house, the owner was threatened by real estate agents and neighbors. She stepped in
and leased the house herself on the understanding with the
owner that she could sub-let it to the evacuees. She lived

with the Japanese American family until the neighbors, through the friendship developed between a little child of the evacuee couple and their own children, began to show genuine friendliness.

Christian student and youth groups also did much to pave the way for the resettlers.

Christian college students were characteristically uneasy about the discriminatory treatment that their fellow students of Japanese ancestry had received. The National Intercollegiate Christian Council, the body that brings all campus Christian associations together, vigorously urged student action in improving student opinion. During the summer months, the N.I.C.C. under the direction of the Y.M.C.A.-Y.W.C.A. Coordinating Committee, and in cooperation with the Protestant Church Commission, sent student workers to the camps to assist in the religious, educational, and recreational activities.

The World Student Service Fund, money-raising agency in the United States sponsored by the World's Student Christian Federation and the International Student Service for student relief throughout the world, "adopted" Nisei student relocation as one of its objectives.

Church boards of education, through their campus representatives, played important parts in opening study opportunities for Nisei and in helping them become adjusted to new campus environments.

Church youth groups learned about the Japanese Americans at summer conferences. Sponsors of these conferences made it a point to invite Nisei to attend them. When Christian youths got acquainted with individual evacuees, they became enthusiastic friends of Japanese Americans.

They went back to their churches and spoke good words about their new friends. Some evacuees, too, actually relocated where their summer acquaintances lived.

The Methodist Youth Fellowship became so interested that it raised enough money among its members to establish a hostel. This hostel served relocating Japanese Americans at Kansas City, Missouri.

But the title of "Fighting Angel" in the story of resettlement goes to individual ministers. Not all ministers went "all out" to help. Some went so completely to war that they refused to have anything to do with the Nisei. However, it was the voice of the pulpit that spoke the first word of Christian fellowship in almost all the communities to which the Japanese Americans came. It was also the ministers to whom relocation officers turned for advice and assistance in the new areas of relocation in routine matters, and in critical situations ministers uniformly rose to the occasion.

For example, Miss Dorothy Brauninger, Youth Worker for the Kansas City Council of Churches, reported that in the fall of 1943, a little six-year-old boy of Japanese ancestry was not permitted to enter the public schools in Kansas City, Kansas. A report was made by a W.R.A. official to the Citizens' Committee, and Dr. W. M. Tippy, a member of that committee, suggested that the Ministerial Alliance in Kansas City, Kansas, be notified, and that each member of the Committee write the daily newspaper. An excellent news story was carried in the paper, and within a few weeks the child was enrolled in the public school.

During the publicity and the discussion of this case, however, Dr. Harold Humbert, then minister of the Central

Christian Church in Kansas City, Kansas, quietly went to the home of the child and invited little Toshio to attend church school with his own little daughter, who was also six years old. Dr. Humbert called for the little boy, and riding together in the car the two children became friends. The child became a favorite in the church school group, and when the public school was finally opened to him, he found himself among friends of his own age.

Miss Brauninger tells of another minister, the Reverend Irvin V. Enos, of the Church of the Brethren, who rented an apartment in his home to a young Nisei couple, only to have his neighbors in the block protest. In spite of threatening letters and telephone calls, Mr. Enos refused to be intimidated, and the young couple remained in his home. A group of young people from the near-by Baptist church called on the young Japanese American couple, took them to a community bowling alley, and welcomed them into the membership and fellowship of their church.

Mr. Francis P. O'Malley of the W.R.A. office in Kansas City, commenting upon these incidents, called the church "a militant body." Elsewhere, as a rule, church people welcomed the evacuees quietly, without publicity.

Mr. William K. Mackay, relocation officer in Columbus, Ohio, spoke of

. . . one of our Christian churches which took a particular interest in a Japanese American family consisting of the father and mother and six children. One of the women's groups of the church arranged a "house-warming" for the family and, as a result, they received many necessary articles of furniture as well as food and clothing.

When the wife of a service man on duty overseas was faced

with the problem of moving her family of four children and all
of their belongings to Columbus from a southern Ohio city,
several men from the North Columbus Friends group hired a
truck, manned it themselves, and moved the entire family.

Still another W.R.A. officer, Mr. George E. Graff, formerly of Detroit, has this story to tell: The Kawamoto
brothers, Mitsuo and Haruo, would often stop in the W.R.A.
office following their day's work at the Michigan Milk Bot-
tle Exchange to chat and to meet other relocatees. On one
summer's afternoon, the two young men inquired of the
relocation officer whether or not there were groups of
young people, that is, Detroit young people, with whom they
might share experiences and have a good time. Mr. Graff
informed them that if they would get a dozen or so young
relocatees to join them, he would see what might be found.
He looked in the classified "ad" section of the telephone
directory and selected at random several churches of whom
he inquired if there were any young people's activities to be
held in the near future. The first four churches that were
called had no activities. A fifth was tried—a group of
young people was to meet a few days hence. The relocation
officer introduced himself and explained what he had hoped
for. The pastor replied that he would do his best to see
that the relocatees "would lose themselves" in the group and
have a good time. Mitsuo, Haruo, and the rest did enjoy
themselves and along with some of the others continued to
go to that church.

Mr. Graff took it upon himself to seek out recreational
opportunities in different churches. One Sunday, he attended the First Presbyterian Church. Listed among the

announcements was the meeting of the Couples' Club during the coming week. The next Monday he talked with the assistant pastor in regard to the possibility of the Nisei sharing an evening with the club. He went with six evacuees. The young people returned to this club throughout the summer to play tennis, ping pong and other games. On any Sunday now one would also find them scattered throughout the congregation.

The churches did more than welcome the evacuees. They were the most effective pioneers in extending full fellowship to them. According to Everett Thompson, the First Methodist Church in Madison, Wisconsin, asked Mrs. Mae Hara to be the choir leader. Mrs. Hara was leader of a prize-winning Japanese American young people's choir in a city-wide choir contest in Seattle a number of years ago, and at Minidoka relocation center trained and led a choir of eighty voices. Mr. Iwao Hara was elected a member of the official board of this church. He is now treasurer of the young married people's club in the church and Mrs. Hara is a member of the church board of education.

This is only one of countless instances. In fact, it is what is happening in most cases where Japanese Americans have joined a local church. Not all of them are contributing as much as do the Haras, but in an ordinary church they have found a sympathetic minister and fair-minded members.

Exceptions are also found. The Susu-Magos, when they moved to Denver, worked among the relocated Nisei there. In their early efforts to integrate the newcomers, they met a few discouraging incidents. They reported that a Nisei girl dropped in to a church service. After worship, the pastor asked her to wait a moment. When he could speak

6

to her alone, he said, "Wouldn't you feel more at home in your own church?"

At another church in Denver where Mr. Susu-Mago took two Nisei girls, one a Buddhist interested in Christ, the pastor promised to have some of his young people call on them, but after a period of weeks no one had been to see the girls. The Nisei minister investigated. He learned that the pastor had told his adult Bible class that "these Japs" were coming to the church only to find out what they could and that if they were admitted to church fellowship, they would soon take over! This man had preached on evangelism that morning, saying that after the war Germany and Japan must be won for Christ.

"Yet one Buddhist American of Japanese descent seemed to present no challenge to him when she appeared on his own doorstep," deplored Mr. Susu-Mago.

In direct contrast to this story is the one of the First Baptist Church in Chicago. The following incident was first told in the *Daily News,* Chicago:

When a Japanese American was employed by a business in Chicago, one of the Caucasian workers was incensed about it. First he objected to the employer, declaring that he would quit the job if the Japanese was not removed. The employer refused to grant his request. Next the man appealed to his fellow employees to strike unless the worker was removed. They refused. Meanwhile, he was seeking a friendly church in Chicago. His search led him to the First Baptist Church one Sunday morning. In the pulpit was the Japanese American associate pastor, the Reverend Jitsuo Morikawa! The worship service and the sermon by Mr. Morikawa convicted the man of sin. He was converted, deep prejudice and hate were uprooted, and he became a new person in Christ. When the deacons asked whom he would like to have baptize him, the new convert could have chosen the Caucasian minister, but he said, "I want to be baptized by Mr. Morikawa." *

It is often said that churches are willing to accept a few members of another race, but when two races try to worship together Sunday after Sunday, it does not work.   Such skeptics will find a different situation at this First Baptist Church in Chicago.   Since Mr. Morikawa came, the membership, both Caucasian and Japanese, has increased.

* Reprinted by permission of *Pastors' Round Table,* Northern Baptist publication.

5

Hostels

Since hostels played an essential rôle in the entire resettlement program, an account of how the hostel was conceived and the functions it performed should be considered.

There was a man named Mr. Thomas Temple at the Manzanar relocation center.[1]   He was with the Community Service section of the W.R.A. administration.   He and the Reverend Ralph E. Smeltzer of the Brethren Service Committee spent many an hour together discussing the evacuee problem.   Mr. Temple, while doing a good job in making life as pleasant as possible for the center residents, could not feel quite satisfied with a well run community.   In fact, the better the interior of the camp became, the more frustrated he felt.   Like many others on the administration, he was convinced that these people should go out and live a normal life.   Mr. Smeltzer heartily agreed.

The rate at which the people were relocating, however, was too low to satisfy them.   Jobs came in, but details were seldom sufficiently described.   Few employment offers were accompanied by housing.   Some evacuees who went out found the jobs unsatisfactory.   Those that stayed on the job had little time to look for permanent living quarters. Some came back to the camp, disappointed.

[1] The material on the origin of the hostel was taken by permission from the B.D. Thesis of Mr. R. A. Burger, Bethany Biblical Seminary.

Mr. Temple and Mr. Smeltzer agreed that the only way to relocate successfully was for the government to permit these people to go out without employment commitment, and for them to have a place where they could stay economically while investigating the most suitable jobs and housing. The answer was the hostel.

In Chicago there is a seminary of the Church of the Brethren, the Bethany Biblical Seminary. Mr. Smeltzer wrote the president of the seminary asking if a part of the dormitory could be used as a relocation hostel. In the meantime, at Manzanar, Mr. Temple and Mr. Smeltzer negotiated with the director of the project while thirteen boys signed up to go if permission was granted.

While the negotiations were in progress, Mr. Smeltzer received a telegram from Bethany Seminary saying that not only would it accommodate the evacuees, but that the students who had heard about the plan had donated sixty dollars to help the evacuees.

The thirteen boys checked out of Manzanar on January 10, 1943, accompanied by Mr. Temple—the first evacuees to leave a relocation center without employment.

The group arrived at Bethany on January 13, and within a few days all of them found satisfactory positions. While at Bethany they lived cooperatively, Mr. Temple acting as manager and house "mother."

Just about this time, another strategy conference was called by the W.R.A. in Chicago to explore new ways of promoting relocation. Representatives of both the American Friends Service Committee and the Brethren Service Committee were present, each with a proposal for a hostel. The hostel plan was adopted, the W.R.A. authorizing these service committees and any other reputable organization to operate hostels and invite evacuees to relocate on "indefinite leave" without prior job offers.

Mr. Temple did not live to see the ongoing work of the hostel, but what he undertook as an experiment became one of the most effective services for relocation, and the word "hostel" became almost a magic word in the relocation centers as the time went on.

In March, 1943, both the Brethren and the Friends Service Committee hostels were operating in Chicago under the direction of Mr. Ralph Smeltzer and Mr. Robertson Fort respectively. Soon the hostels proved to be indispensable. In them more than five thousand evacuees were served.

Subsequently additional hostels were operated through 1943 and 1944 in Des Moines, Cleveland, Cincinnati, Washington, D. C., Detroit, Philadelphia, and Minneapolis.[2]

The hostel was a hub of activities. Applications for lodging from the centers were received by mail. Upon approval, an official invitation was sent. This was necessary for an evacuee to secure a leave certificate. When the hostel received word as to the time the evacuee would arrive, the director went to the station to meet him. The newcomer became a cooperative member of the "family." He received an orientation course about the city. From the hostel he went out with "leads" both for employment and more permanent housing. The director was always ready to listen and counsel.

Thus at the hostel the evacuee cast off his initial fear of the outside world. It was the link between the camp and the community. For this very important service he paid

[2] For complete list of hostels, see Appendix, p. 145.

for board and room—usually not more than a dollar and a half a day. The hostels welcomed all evacuees regardless of religion.

Though it was feared at first that they might become objects of assault as "Jap houses," those hostels were opened without any serious difficulty. But when the Brethren Service Committee decided to close its hostel in Chicago and move it to New York, a "national battle" ensued over it. It is the now famous Brooklyn Hostel. But for its full story, let us ask Dr. J. Henry Carpenter, executive secretary of the Brooklyn Church and Mission Federation, to tell us the "day-to-day" developments to show how the church fought its way to a moral victory, a conspicuous highlight in the history of resettlement. This is what happened:

The plans for opening the hostel in New York unfortunately, or fortunately, came at just the time a flare-up had occurred in New Jersey. A farmer living in Great Meadows, New Jersey, had hired four Issei farmers to work for him. Neighboring farmers objected to the "influx" of Japanese into their community. Actually they were fearful of economic competition, but based their argument on mistrust of all Japanese. The farmer, who refused to discharge his helpers, found fires started in his outbuildings and other threats of violence on the part of other farmers. All of this was carried in the papers in scare headlines. This really was the first publicity in the East revealing that these evacuees were coming to this part of the country. Although the actual facts proved that the basis of the struggle was a feud-like situation between Polish and Russian immigrants who were farming these lands, and that the coming of the Japanese farmers was only the incident that started the conflagration, the harm was done. In the newspapers and public eye the whole question was the coming of the Japanese American evacuees to the East. The fact that these men were not all American citizens was widely heralded.

Governor Edge entered the controversy with a statement that the Japanese Americans were not welcome in New Jersey. So-called patriotic groups took up the cry and passed resolutions about the danger of sabotage and other dire results if these "Japs" were allowed to come to the East Coast where they could spy on shipping, etc. The reactionaries won out temporarily, and to silence the controversy the men were quietly sent to another location by the W.R.A. Although there probably would have been real difficulty in any case, this New Jersey case coming just before the opening of the New York Hostel greatly aggravated the struggle that developed. People's minds were, so to speak, opened to the "evils" of having these evacuees coming to the East Coast.

The story of selecting the site for the New York Hostel and the final decision to locate in Brooklyn can best be told by the following quotation from an article by the Reverend Ralph Smeltzer, which appeared in the *Gospel Messenger,* a Church of the Brethren publication, for August 12, 1944. Mr. Smeltzer wrote:

After investigating various eastern areas and discussing the matter with Washington W.R.A. officials, New York City was decided upon. Mr. George Rundquist of the Committee on Resettlement, the New York Church Committee, Mr. Harold S. Fistere of the W.R.A., Dr. John W. Thomas of the American Baptist Home Mission Society, and Dr. J. Henry Carpenter promised the support of their respective organizations in establishing a New York relocation hostel. It was difficult to find a suitable house. Possible locations were investigated in Manhattan, Brooklyn, Queens, and Westchester County. Finally, it was decided to concentrate the search in Brooklyn. After several fruitless days of searching, it was decided to telephone the various fraternities' houses in the hope that one might be leased for a year. Alpha Chi Rho, the fourth one contacted, was interested. Negotiations began on March 31. On April 3, Dr. J. Quinter Miller of the Federal Council of Churches, Dr. John W. Thomas, and Mr. Smeltzer secured a tentative lease approval from three fraternity officials. The lease terms were drawn up to become effective May 1. The transaction could not be completed at once because, according to the fraternity's by-laws, both its national board of directors and its building corporation members had to approve by majority vote.

The Alpha Chi house is located at 168 Clinton Street, Brooklyn, which is in the downtown Brooklyn Heights area. Every attempt was made to keep the negotiations quiet, but eventually the newspapers got a "hot tip." The Brooklyn *Eagle* editors immediately called the Brooklyn Church and Mission Federation office and stated that if the true and accurate story was not given, there was no limit to what the newspapers might print. Although agreement had been reached in the Committee on Resettlement and the W.R.A. to give out no information, the danger of adverse news made up by unofficial reporters seemed extremely hazardous. Therefore the minimum story was given to the *Eagle* by Mr. Rundquist. This story and a picture of the house appeared in the *Eagle* on April 16, 1944. The following appeared under the picture: "Home for Evacuees— Negotiations now under way may transform this Clinton

Street building from a fraternity house to a hostel for Japanese Americans moved out of West Coast military areas." The article stated:

A Brooklyn interfaith committee, with Catholic and Jewish representation, as well as members of the Brooklyn Church and Mission Federation and the Salvation Army, will foster the work, which is to provide housing for evacuees. The work is being encouraged by the War Relocation Authority, a federal body. Plans for the opening have been laid quietly. Mr. Rundquist pointed out that such hostels under church sponsorship have the best chance of doing a good job. "The church sponsorship," he said, "encourages the evacuee, who might otherwise be fearful of discrimination or even of hurt. A better job of adjustment can be done."

The article was rewritten and appeared in the New York Times on April 19. This set the stage for a controversy reflected in newspapers across the country. Most New York newspapers took an editorial position in favor of the hostel and the relocation program. Mention of the controversy appeared in some New York City newspaper every day for a month—April 24 to May 22. The newspaper PM plugged the hardest for the hostel.

In the initial stage it was felt best to form a Brooklyn-wide interfaith and inter-agency committee to help in the work of the hostel. The interest of the Brooklyn Church and Mission Federation officials was taken up by the Salvation Army, the Y.W.C.A., and many other church and social agencies. As an interfaith approach it was decided to take the question to the Brooklyn Council for Social Planning, which has eighty-six member agencies of all faiths. Miss Helen Currier, the executive secretary, was very cooperative. It was unanimously agreed by the board of directors of the Brooklyn Council on Tuesday, April 11, to form an interfaith committee. The responsibility for forming the committee was left to the chairman, Mr. Mortimer Brenner, and the secretaries of the Council and the Church Federation. It was decided that no one of the "expected" or "naturals" should be the chairman, but that a prominent Catholic laymen should be selected. As there was no great hurry about selecting the full committee personnel, only a tentative list had been decided upon up to Friday, April 21.

On this day, a different tip came to the local Federation office. Local citizens, alarmed by the prospects of an inroad of "Japanese saboteurs" into the Heights area, had met and, as Mr. Smeltzer relates, prepared the following petition: "We, the undersigned, property owners in the vicinity of 168 Clinton Street, Brooklyn, New York, strongly object to a hostel for Japanese being opened. . . . " It was circulated in the neighborhood by a small boy who allegedly obtained one hundred and thirty-six signatures, many of which were not those of property owners.

This petition was taken to the Honorable John T. Delaney, the Congressman from the district, in Washington. Congressman Delaney became alarmed and promised immediate action. He visited Mr. Dillon S. Myer, director of the W.R.A., and protested vigorously against the hostel's establishment. Because of this "tip," the Council decided upon immediate action and to fight hard for justice and the rights of these Japanese Americans. The papers did not get this story until April 24. In the meantime, by working on Saturday and Sunday, the Council sent a letter calling a meeting of the committee on Tuesday. Monsignor Jerome J. Reedy of the Catholic Charities had been contacted and had suggested the name of Supreme Court Justice William F. Hagarty as the chairman. Judge Hagarty fitted every description. He was prominent. He was not a "natural." He was a Heights citizen, living around the corner from the proposed hostel, and he was a Catholic layman. His consent was secured. The committee was formed. On Monday, April 24, the report of the action of Heights citizens and their petition to Congressman Delaney "broke" in the *Eagle*. The *Times* printed it the next morning, but because of the immediate action taken by the Council both articles listed the very prominent members of the interfaith committee appointed by the council. This took the edge off what might otherwise have been a very unfavorable newspaper story.

The next day, the committee met at the Council headquarters, and residents of the local area, though uninvited, came to the meeting. Mr. Harold S. Fistere and other representatives of the W.R.A. office were present, as well as members of the New York Church Committee. The city newspapers had reporters at the meeting. As Judge Hagarty, who had accepted the chairmanship, could not be present, the meeting was presided over by Mr. Mortimer Brenner, the president of the Council. With the background of a prominent attorney, Mr. Brenner carried forward the meeting with fairness, calmness, and dispatch. He welcomed the "guests" and assured them they would have their chance to talk. He announced that Judge Hagarty had accepted the chairmanship of the committee and that he and Dr. Carpenter were elected vice-chairmen.

The *Eagle* the next day printed a detailed story of the

proceedings. To give as complete a picture as possible here, this story is reproduced:

A committee to foster the interests of Japanese Americans in a Brooklyn hostel was functioning today with Associate Justice William F. Hagarty of the Appellate Division as chairman. Despite objections voiced by a number of Brooklyn Heights residents at the first meeting of the committee called together by the Brooklyn Council for Social Planning yesterday, the committee proceeded with its business, Mortimer Brenner, president of the Council and chairman of the meeting, announcing that a resolution in favor of the project was carried.

In answer to questions put by Councilman Genevieve Earle, a member of the committee, George E. Rundquist of the Committee on Resettlement of Japanese Americans said the location at 168 Clinton street was all but settled and he hoped to hear within a few days that the lease had been signed.

Between forty and fifty men and women attended the meeting, with a large majority favoring the hostel. This did not prevent their opponents, a number of whom had not been invited, from being permitted to state their objections.

[They] agreed in principle with the idea of aiding the Japanese American evacuees, but opposed the establishment on Clinton Street, holding that the street was a busy one and the location too prominent for a building which would come to be known as "that Japanese house." [One of them] held that many truck loads of soldiers passed the house each day, often on their way overseas, and that the trucks had to stop at a traffic light directly in front of the house. [Another] opposed the idea flatly. "I am not altogether sure I want to live with the Japanese," he said. "I am paying taxes up to the hilt. I have one son overseas and another about to enter the service. And now my home is being jeopardized. I think it is unfair to cause property in this neighborhood to deteriorate. I am a little bit concerned about our boys who are coming back every day now and who have no place to sleep. Why not a hostel for our own boys? You can go to our big hotels and find the boys sleeping on blankets while the big gathering rooms are empty. I'm at war with the Japanese. I want to do a little bit more for our own before we go afield. This talk about Americanism of this and that is used to cover too many things. Let us remove the beam from our own eyes."

Dr. J. Henry Carpenter, secretary of the Brooklyn Church and Mission Federation, answered [this person], calling attention to the Japanese Americans fighting in the United States forces in Italy.

Dr. Phillips Packer Elliot of the First Presbyterian Church, who was present, the Reverend John Howland Lathrop of the Church of the Savior, not present but a member of the committee, and the Reverend William Howard Melish of the Church of the Holy Trinity, present and a member, are all members of the board of governors.

Mr. Harold S. Fistere explained that the evacuees had been sent to relocation centers in mountain and western states after Pearl Harbor, that about 70 per cent were native Americans and the rest had been in this country from twenty to forty years. Half of them were Christians, he said, with the balance Buddhists who participated freely in Christian functions.

The W.R.A., while interested in seeing such movements as the Brooklyn Hostel established, had no authority in the matter, he said. Its financial obligation was limited to providing the evacuees with day coach tickets from their center to whatever place they picked out for settlement, plus three dollars a day for meals and twenty-five dollars in cash.

Mr. Melish read to the committee and observers a leading editorial in the Brooklyn *Eagle* yesterday indorsing the idea of the hostel. Mr. Brenner, in calling the meeting to order, announced Justice Hagarty's acceptance of the chairmanship but explained he could not be present due to court duties. He then said: "The purpose of this committee is not to foster or propose a hostel in Clinton Street. It may be this decision will come later. Our purpose is much broader. A challenge has come to the people of Brooklyn. We in Brooklyn must not be found guilty of the excesses that do occur in other parts of the country.

"As a result of the war emergency, the Japanese Americans have been called upon to make greater sacrifices than any others. Not only have their sons gone to war, but those who lived on the West Coast have been required to abandon their homes and businesses and to live under government supervision before relocating themselves in strange cities.

"Fewer than two thousand are to be brought to Brooklyn, a city of three million people. We should be able to take them in without even noticing it. We should be able to help them readjust themselves without unpleasant or sensational occurrences. This not only would be preaching democracy but living up to it."

The Reverend Alfred L. Scott, pastor of the Church of the Nazarene, spoke of the danger of incurring the same kind of incident in Brooklyn which occurred when four Japanese were taken by a farmer to work in Great Meadows, New Jersey.

Dr. Elliott urged that the committee go beyond an endorsement of the principle involved and take a stand in favor of the hostel wherever it is located in Brooklyn. "To approve the principle and not the application would be futile," he added.

While these meetings were taking place, other opposition groups were working also. Mayor LaGuardia in a front page article in the *Times* on Wednesday was reported as filing with the Army, Navy, and other agencies in Washington a vigorous protest against the relocation of Japanese Americans in New York City or in any of the states on the eastern seaboard. Although the mayor remained silent on the subject, it is known that his opposition was registered several weeks previously. The W.R.A. officials immediately contacted Washington when the mayor's story was released, and went directly to Secretary Ickes. The next day the papers carried a statement by the Secretary of the Interior as follows:

Within the past two weeks, the American people have heard three high public officials giving voice to opinions that seem ominously out of tune in a nation that is fighting for the principles of democracy and freedom.

First the governor of New Jersey, then the governor of Ohio, and now, of all people, the mayor of New York City, have expressed a belief that American citizens of Japanese ancestry and law-abiding Japanese aliens are not entitled to the same privileges as non-Japanese and should be accorded special treatment. This is a strange fife and drum corps to be playing the discordant anthem of racial discrimination. Stranger by far than fiction. The mayor of New York City, who has fought long and vigorously for racial equality and justice, carrying the flag, must be shocked and disturbed to find the drummer boy from New Jersey on his left and the fifer from Ohio flanking him on the right. I cannot but believe that he has joined this company through accident and misunderstanding rather than by deliberate choice.

Mayor LaGuardia has protested against the relocation of persons of Japanese ancestry in New York City, apparently on the theory that these people are dangerous and subversive. Actually there has not been one proved case of sabotage on the part of a Japanese American since the war began, not even in Hawaii.

I have no hesitancy in saying that an overwhelming majority of the American public, firm believers in fair play and the Constitution, hold no animosity against these homeless and blameless victims of a wartime military decision. As an indication of this, even in the Far West, I should like to call attention to an assembly of more than five hundred girls from ten Arizona high schools who met at Rivers, Arizona, on April 15, with Japanese American schoolgirls from the W.R.A.

Gila River, Arizona, project to discuss in a spirit of tolerance and good will their mutual problems.

To me such a meeting spells anything but racial intolerance. To me it is indicative of the way the vast majority of our citizens feel, once they have the facts, toward those of Japanese descent, Governors Bricker and Edge and Mayor LaGuardia notwithstanding. Little children shall lead them.

On the same day political leaders were contacted in Brooklyn and a call was put through to Washington to the Congressman involved, as he was the person who actually gave the mayor's statement to the press. From that time on, neither the mayor nor the Congressman made any further statements.

Resolutions against the hostel also were passed by the Kings County American Legion, the Veterans of Foreign Wars, New York City Woman's Clubs, and some twenty other organizations. This was countered, however, by more than thirty resolutions by church and civic organizations. The Y.W.C.A., Bishop James P. DeWolfe for the Episcopal Diocese, the Salvation Army, the Brooklyn Church and Mission Federation, the Boro President's Committee on Racial Understanding, and other denominational and social agencies all voted strong and favorable action.

There are two more parts of this story that should be told, however, "for the record." The first is the actual rental of the hostel from the fraternity, and the second, the meeting when the actual decision was made to open the hostel. All of these events so overlapped each other it is almost impossible to give a completely chronological story of what happened.

The question of the rental of the Alpha Chi Rho fra-

7

ternity house, though agreed to by the local organization, had to be finally approved, as mentioned before, by the national office of the fraternity. Because so much discussion and tension had developed, there was a real question as to whether the national group would give approval. Thus the whole matter might have been stopped at this point. On the same night that this national committee was meeting, a special session of the executives of the Brooklyn Heights Association was also called. Because these two meetings conflicted and because of the vital importance of favorable action by both bodies, it was decided that Mr. Fistere and Mr. Rundquist should go to the Heights Association meeting and that Mr. Smeltzer and the secretary of the Brooklyn Church and Mission Federation should go to the fraternity meeting. Arrangements for telephone connection at certain intervals were made so that one decision might influence the other. Mr. Smeltzer is again quoted as to the results of these two gatherings:

After several postponements, the fraternity officials finally arranged to meet on the evening of May 2. Their decision was doubtful, the situation critical. Answers to these questions were needed: Would the fraternity vote for the lease? Should the lease be accepted if offered? Would there be violence in the neighborhood? Should the hostel idea be given up? Four national board members, including a Congressman and a Navy officer, four local fraternity directors, two fraternity house residents, and one inter-fraternity representative gathered for the decision. Dr. Miller, Dr. Carpenter, and the writer represented the Brethren Service Committee. A fine-spirited letter from the fraternity's lawyer was read. The fraternity men considered the matter carefully, voted to lease their house, guaranteed the hostel their genuine support. Additional drama was added to the meeting when it was reported that the board of governors of the Brooklyn Heights Association, a community betterment organization of the hostel neighborhood, had a few minutes earlier passed the following resolution: "Resolved, that the Brooklyn Heights Association views with interest the proposal to establish a Japanese American Relocation Hostel on Brooklyn Heights, and that a committee of five be appointed as an advisory committee to cooperate with the authorities sponsoring the project." Thus the renting of the hostel was confirmed and the Heights Association had made an almost unanimous vote to cooperate with the hostel.

It should be noted here that three ministerial members of the Heights Association did yeoman service. They were Dr. John Howland Lathrop of the Unitarian Church, Dr. Phillips P. Elliott of the First Presbyterian Church, and the Reverend William Howard Melish of the Holy Trinity Episcopal Church. All of these men also served on the hostel committee. Another incident that happened at that meeting should be mentioned. A captain in the Navy who was a member of the association voted against the final motion, but laconically explained his vote by saying, "I will not vote for such a weak resolution. Why don't you come right out and condemn these rabble-rousing and un-American activities and agree to unlimited support in every possible way of the hostel and Japanese Americans coming to our city?"

With all these battles won, there was still doubt in the minds of the leaders as to whether they should open the hostel. The climactic meeting was a comparatively small one and was held in the office of the Federal Council of Churches. There had been a suggestion of violence. Even setting fire to the hostel or accosting individual Japanese Americans on the streets had been threatened. Was there actual possibility of this or was it mere loud talk? After all, were Mr. and Mrs. Smeltzer to go there alone and open up the place and stand the consequences?

Those who met were Dr. Roswell P. Barnes, Dr. J. Quinter Miller, Mr. George E. Rundquist, for the Federal Council; Mr. Harold S. Fistere for the W.R.A.; the Reverend and Mrs. Ralph Smeltzer and Miss Muriel Ferguson for the hostel; Mr. Mortimer Brenner, Dr. Robert W. Searle, and the secretary of the Brooklyn Church and Mission Federation for the local committees. As we look back on it, it seems almost surprising, in view of later events, that there was so much question. Yet it was a real decision that had to be made. Mr. Fistere turned to the Smeltzers and said, "Are you willing to take the chances of even bodily harm which might result?" Both answered calmly and determinedly, "Yes, we have faced it and are willing."

Again Mr. Fistere suggested that the first night would be the most difficult. If we could get by the first two or three nights without difficulty, the hostel would be assured. To back down now would affect the whole resettlement program on the entire eastern seaboard. Finally, after certain leaders volunteered to be at the hostel, so as not to have the Smeltzers alone at dangerous hours, a vote was taken by poling each person in the room individually. It was unanimously decided to open the hostel.

Mr. Smeltzer tells of this event in the following words:

With the hostel assured and the fight won, the Smeltzers moved in May 5. The first hostelers arrived on schedule, May 10. Newsmen and photographers greeted them. Early arrivals and interested friends helped make the hostel ready for full occupancy. Friends donated needed articles. The Arts Council of Japanese Americans for Democracy hung an exhibit of its paintings. Gradually the number of hostelers was increased to capacity—twenty-five. Next-door neighbors are congenial. Hostelers go about the neighborhood without fear or embarrassment. The hostel has received no protests. No unfriendly acts have come to the hostel's attention. To all appearances the hostel has been completely accepted. The local precinct police captain frequently visits the hostel informally and in plain clothes. He is sympathetic and interested in helping the project succeed. During the early days he asked his man who regularly patrols this area to give more attention to the hostel. For a few days a uniformed policeman posted himself very close to the hostel, sometimes directly in front. After a week's time, his beat was enlarged to a block or two. Now at times he can nowhere be seen.

The battle was completely won through quick action. Faith in brotherhood and freedom for all people was completely vindicated.

6

The Church Takes Political Action in Colorado

COLORADO has held a unique place among the intermountain states since Pearl Harbor. When the evacuation was still on a voluntary basis, and hostility was mounting against the voluntary evacuees who moved into Colorado, the Honorable Ralph L. Carr, then governor of Colorado, declared: "If we do not extend humanity's kindness and understanding to these people, if we deny them the protection of the Bill of Rights, if we say they may be denied the privilege of living in any of the forty-eight states without hearing or charge of misconduct, then we are tearing down the whole American system."

The Colorado Council of Churches issued the following statement in early summer, 1942:

Historically, all religions have taught that behind the mask which we place upon people is the universal brotherhood of man. The churches have a duty to Japanese Americans. These Japanese Americans are well disposed to following the teachings of Christianity and to assume their citizenship responsibilities. We must start practising the gospel we have preached. We must start molding public opinion and cease lip service. There are one-half million or more in this state to whom politicians will listen if the church decides to become vocal and do something. If the church does not, it will deserve the indictment which those less cognizant of its creed of brotherhood would be glad to pronounce over it.

The Denver Council of Churches and the Colorado Council of Churches, the Denver Y.W.C.A., and other organizations have committees working on this program. Several committees have been appointed and many clergymen and laymen have shown a profound concern over the welfare of evacuees. Few instances have been reported of animosity by church groups to this problem. Notable is the case of a small church in the state which excluded evacuees from membership. What is necessary is the definite concerted action of all groups.

The issue must be faced. Democracy will go down first of all on the rocks of racial prejudice and discrimination. We cannot wait until the war is over. For one of the fundamental issues in this world-wide war is that of race equality or inequality. We see it in Europe with the Nazi emphasis on the superior race. We see it in Asia, in Japan, in China, in India. We cannot wait—the crisis is upon us. It is upon our world—whether the white people of the earth, who themselves are a minority, are willing to know it or not. Will it be again a question of "too little democracy on our part—and too late"?

We must move swiftly and at once. We must see to it that Americans shall have equal economic opportunity and that colored people in this democracy shall not suffer insult because of their color. . . . Is democracy right or is it wrong? If it is right, then let us dare to make it true.

Can you begin with yourself, asking such questions as "How do I feel about the Japanese, the Negro, the Spanish-speaking? Am I willing that they should work with me, live in my neighborhood, and go to my church?" [1]

There were only 2,671 Japanese in Colorado prior to December 7, 1941, of whom 862 were citizens. Since Pearl Harbor, 2,343 have relocated in that state by voluntary evacuation; 1,598 of these were citizens. In two years,

[1] From the pamphlet *The Japanese in Our Midst.* Colorado Council of Churches, 1942.

about three thousand evacuees relocated from the relocation centers.

The residents of Colorado were "alarmed," and one of the most significant political battles resulted. One state senator said, "This might be the point on which our country would break." The Reverend Clark P. Garman, formerly a Congregational missionary in Japan, and now minister to Japanese under the Colorado Council of Churches, who also was executive secretary of the Colorado Committee for Fair Play, the organization that carried the fight to the voters, tells the story on what the churches did, as follows:

In January, 1944, pressure was put on Governor Vivian to call a special session of the legislature to consider placing on the November ballot an amendment that would deny to aliens ineligible to citizenship the right to own property in the state. The clamor for this came from Adams County, where the largest Japanese population resides, with backing from some other parts of the state. After conference with both proponents and opponents, the governor acquiesced. Due study of the proposal by the legislature was made—including an open hearing at which representatives of both sides presented their viewpoints. The proposal before the legislature was not that of denying alien ownership, but only whether such decision should be referred to the electorate. It failed to carry.

Immediately following the session of the legislature, a petition was circulated to secure sufficient names to place the proposal before the electorate by this method. This was easily done. The proponents incorporated as the "American League," and what became Amendment No. 3 appeared on the ballot as follows:

An Act amending Section 27 of Article II of the Constitution of Colorado [2] to Provide that Aliens eligible to Citizenship may acquire, hold and dispose of Real and Personal Property. Also that Provision shall be made by Law for the Right and Power of Aliens ineligible to Citizenship to acquire, hold and dispose of Real Property; otherwise there shall be no such right or power as to them, directly or indirectly, except as to Vested Rights already acquired and guaranteed by Law, which rights may be dissolved, liquidated or terminated also by Law.

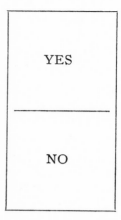

YES

NO

If this amendment was adopted, the clause beginning "otherwise" would become effective immediately, thus denying the Filipinos, Koreans, and immigrants from India, as well as the Japanese, the rights accorded German or Italian aliens. But the real issue, exaggerated a hundred times, was whether alien Japanese should be allowed to purchase real property. Contrary to the public's misconception, in all Colorado there were only 146 farmers of Japanese ancestry who owned their land, of whom 82 were citizens. The contention that "Japs are buying up our fair land" was actually based upon the purchase of land by *seven* newcomers.

As the opposition gathered strength a nucleus of opponents to the proposal developed within the legislature and without. This was made up of representatives of various

[2] Section 27 of Article II, "Property Rights of Aliens." Aliens, who are or may hereafter become bona fide residents of this state, may acquire, inherit, possess, enjoy, dispose of property, real and personal, as native citizens. Adopted in 1876. AUTHOR'S NOTE: Eligibility to citizenship was not conditional.

groups—religious, civic, educators, lawyers, and others. A hastily formed Citizens' Emergency Committee circulated a statement in opposition to placing the proposal on the ballot. Later, those in the Denver area held informal meetings to consider the advisability of unitedly opposing the proposed amendment. There was much doubt regarding the possibility of defeating the amendment, but the fifty or so attending the series of meetings decided that an attempt should be made. A program was adopted, and an executive committee appointed.

The necessity of assembling and publishing factual data was recognized. This task was facilitated by a fairly comprehensive survey by the Denver office of the W.R.A. covering population, property, ownership, etc., of Colorado residents of Japanese ancestry. It also was recognized that the fundamental issue at stake was the maintenance of the principles and practices upon which America was founded. This resulted in the adoption of the slogan: "Keep Colorado American; Vote 'No' on Amendment No. 3."

The Executive Committee incorporated, with prominent representatives from different parts of the state as directors. President R. G. Gustavson of Colorado University was made honorary chairman. The names thus added gave prestige to the Committee and assisted greatly in securing the large number of sponsors from various parts of the state. Local activity was promoted in a number of cities and towns, and, where possible, branch committees were formed. For this purpose, visits were made to Pueblo, Colorado Springs, Lamar, Rocky Ford, Grand Junction, Delta, and elsewhere. Correspondence was continuous with representatives in Denver and in other cities. A Larimer County committee was formed, with H. H. Wright of Fort Collins as secretary, and with other officers who were leading educators in the county.

The financial problem loomed large when the Executive Committee took over. Its activities were necessarily limited by the funds available, and could be planned only as receipts were in hand or in sight. A few organizations offered aid. These included the Denver Y.W.C.A. and the American Association of Social Workers. Great encouragement came from the Council of Social Action of the Congregational Christian Churches, which donated a large fund and lent the services of Mr. Galen R. Weaver for two months, with salary and travel to and from Colorado. Another large gift was received from a private source. Other contributions were made by the United Christian Missionary Society and the Colorado Missionary Society (both organizations of the Disciples of Christ).

The enrollment of sponsors was an important part of the publicity campaign. Decision was made by many who had previously given little or no thought to the amendment. As the roll of sponsors composed of leading citizens increased, its influence on the general public was cumulative.

Speakers addressed many gatherings in churches, service clubs, and the like. Special forums and public meetings were arranged. The outstanding speaker in the campaign was Mr. Weaver, who accepted invitations in Denver, Pueblo, Colorado Springs, Montrose, Longmont, Loveland, Fort Collins, and Greeley. Both his ability as a thinker and a speaker and his background eminently fitted him for this work. Long residence in Honolulu, attendance at the biennial sessions of the Institute of Pacific Relations, presence in Honolulu prior to, at the time of, and after the Pearl Harbor disaster—these combined to prepare him both as a narrator and an interpreter of the facts Coloradans were anxious to know at this juncture. His addresses well illustrated the fact that the discriminatory measure placed before the voters of Colorado was but a small part of a national and international problem that did not originate and will not end in the state.

The Committee was fortunate, also, in securing for two days the services of Mr. Carey McWilliams, former Coloradan, attorney, writer, and lecturer, who has given much thought and research to America's racial problems, including the issues centering about Japanese immigrants and their descendants.

Radio and newspaper publicity was given greatest emphasis. Press notices and interviews were arranged. Four-inch "ads" were run in Colorado's one hundred and seventy-one daily and weekly newspapers, and in the racial and religious organs available.

The original pressure on Governor Vivian by Adams County legislators was seemingly brought at the request of truck farmers, largely of Italian descent. The mayor of Brighton became head of the "American League." He was the main speaker at forums and public meetings in the Denver area until near the end of October. Then he was joined by Mr. John R. Lechner, associated with California anti-Japanese activities, who participated in public meetings at Brighton, Grand Junction, and Denver. Advertisements were run in the Grand Junction *Sentinel* and Denver *Post*. The *Post* also carried an interview with Mr. Lechner, under the heading: "Expert Says Jap Land-Owners Drive Out

American Farmers." The Denver *Post* recommended a "Yes" vote on the amendment.

The Rocky Mountain News and the Pueblo *Star Journal* and *Chieftain* opposed the amendment. It was also opposed, with reasons, by both the Colorado State League of Women Voters and the Denver Civic League, as well as by the *Intermountain Jewish News,* the *Colorado Statesman* and the *Star* (both Negro papers), and the *Rocky Mountain Churchman.* The Fellowship of Reconciliation, the Cosmopolitan Club, the Japanese American Citizens League, the Farmers' Union, the Colorado Council of Churches and Colorado Council of Church Women, the Denver Council of Churches and Denver Council of Church Women, and many other Denver organizations also opposed the amendment.

The outcome of the campaign, however, remained in the balance as the day of voting approached. No one on the committee could predict, and many were actually pessimistic. But when the votes were cast and the committee members sat in waiting, feeling that they had done the best they could, a great surprise greeted them as the votes were gradually tabulated, precinct by precinct.

In Denver, the Negro and Jewish precincts voted "No." Italian and Spanish districts voted "Yes." Montrose County reported "No" led by a 1,000 vote majority! In Pueblo County the amendment was defeated by two to one. In Grand Junction the soldier vote was just as strongly opposed as the county was for it. The soldier vote was in fact most encouraging everywhere, refuting the argument of the proponents of the amendment that the fighting men would not tolerate their land being bought up by the "Japs" while they were defending it overseas. Even in Denver, where the civilian votes were "Yes," the soldiers voted "No." This was true also in Adams and Mesa counties.

It was evident that the somewhat confusing wording of the amendment created less confusion than had been feared, for there were two other amendments to be voted upon and only Amendment No. 3 was voted down.

The battle was won. Colorado remained "American," as the Committee's slogan suggested.

Mr. Dillon S. Myer, director of the W.R.A., wrote to Mr. Garman: "I congratulate you personally, and the Colorado Committee for Fair Play, Inc., for the job that the Committee has done for Colorado. It goes to prove that a small group of good people with a good cause, who really put forth an effort, can do what to many people would seem impossible."

7

Church Life in Evolution

I N the previous chapters we have seen instances of local churches accepting evacuees as members. But as the number of resettlers increased with a growing general public acceptance, not all former members of the Japanese churches found their way into Caucasian churches in the communities to which they went.

Councils of churches and ministers on the West Coast, particularly returned Caucasian missionaries who worked among the Japanese people in camp, provided relocating Japanese Americans with letters of introduction. Evacuee ministers in the centers did likewise. The Manzanar Project office regularly sent to the Committee on Resettlement of Japanese Americans lists of relocating Christian persons, indicating their denominational affiliations and destinations. The Committee in turn notified the local churches. The Protestant Church Commission vigorously followed up relocatees lest they lose contact with the churches. Still the majority of the Christian evacuees did not join the local churches. There are many factors responsible for this.

Once the cohesive adherence of members to the original church was broken up by the evacuation, nothing replaced the original church to claim their loyalty. Federated churches in the centers were necessarily stop-gaps. While the cooperation among various denominations was praiseworthy and much valuable experience was gained by both clergy and laity, church life without a denominational basis was not normal.

Before we judge, therefore, the success or failure of the individual initiative of the evacuee to make the transfer "from his all-Japanese church in a relocation center to the nearest church of his denomination in the community," it is necessary for us to appreciate the effect of the camp life upon the people.

In the relocation centers the federation of the churches was effected by necessity, first by the order of the military, and then by the suggestion of the W.R.A. Church members, leaders, ministers, and missionaries all agreed generally that it was the best and only way under the circumstances.

Thus in the federated church, events unlikely under normal conditions took place.

Miss Anna Bell Williams, a returned Methodist missionary at the Rohwer relocation center, expressed appreciation when she wrote:

When a new member is received, the pastor of the group to which the person had some previous affiliation baptizes either by immersion or sprinkling, as the case may be. It is inspiring to see the Baptist minister hold the bowl of water for the Presbyterian. About eighty were baptized the first Easter Sunday of center life. The joy of taking communion together, where all are one in Christ Jesus, with no distinction, cannot be understood by those who have never had nor desired such an experience.

The impact of common suffering stretched this spirit of cooperation far beyond all possible imagination under any other circumstances. In order fully to understand the relocating Christian's attitude to the church outside, this unique background of center experience must be borne in mind. We quote from a letter from the Reverend Abe, the Congregational minister:

At Manzanar, where the mountains are high and the water is clear, we organized a federated church program. There were nine Protestant ministers, three Catholic priests, and four Buddhist priests, but only three churches—one Protestant, one Catholic, and one Buddhist. The Buddhists had four sects, Nichiren, Shinshu, Zen, and Kohya. The W.R.A. wanted us to unite our efforts, thus contributing to the harmony and morale of the camps. We were given buildings for religious services and enjoyed freedom of worship within the centers.

Not only did the denominations of each faith act together, but the three faiths cooperated. We held joint conferences on general moral discipline, family problems, etc. Memorial services for Nisei service men killed in action were held under joint sponsorship.

When Christmas came with its surprise presents, all groups worked together to make the Advent a time of celebration by the entire community. America as a Christian nation established her good name in the heart of every resident.

As we have maintained a federated church here at Manzanar, our members are ready to join a church of any denomination when they go out. How much freer we should feel if the churches in America were all united so that we could integrate fully into the life of the American churches!

The point made is clear. The evacuees who have worshiped in an interdenominational church do not show the same enthusiasm towards our denominations that we do.

As the tempo of relocation increased the evacuees began to enjoy a social life among themselves outside. This was natural. Working and living day by day among Caucasians

8

had both pleasant and nerve-straining features. Life in the relocation centers conditioned most evacuees to keep to themselves. Consequently, being among their Japanese friends had an element of relief and relaxation that no one who has not gone through the evacuation can fully appreciate. For most evacuees, therefore, going to church was not a simple matter of going to a place of worship. It was, by and large, going to a *Caucasian* church.

If no one paid any attention to them there, they did not know whether they were being politely ignored or just plain unwelcome. Being ignored is usually the experience of most church-goers at large churches in large cities. And large cities are where the majority of the evacuees relocated.

But if a well-meaning minister, who had a letter of introduction, changed his voice while making the usual announcements, and said, "Friends, this morning we have a Christian witness to the brotherhood of man. Mr. and Mrs. Goto from a Japanese camp are worshiping with us. How wonderful it is that in time of war we can share the fellowship of Christ with Japanese friends! I hope you will get acquainted with them after the service, and Mr. and Mrs. Goto, I welcome you to our church," the Gotos might or might not return to that church, depending upon whether they felt genuinely welcomed or merely conspicuous.

Furthermore, the wartime migration of people was so large in number that local churches, except where united efforts were employed deliberately to seek out church members among new residents, were not able to cope with the shifting population. It has been generally acknowledged among leaders of the churches that it takes from three to twelve months before a newcomer to a community is brought into the fellowship of a church. The evacuees were no exception.

How, then, should the church deal with this problem of the church life of the Japanese Americans? Should the church leave them alone, hoping that in due time they will find a church where they will feel at home? Or, should separate churches be provided for them as in pre-war days? If we take the first course, there is a risk of losing Christians. If the latter course is adopted, more Japanese will be "churched," but at the risk of segregation within the church.

As the relocation center churches were gradually reduced in membership, the mission bodies of the churches wrestled with this question, desperately seeking an answer.

Mr. Ralph Smeltzer, who was one of the most fervent believers in the integration of Japanese Americans through the churches, offers the following account of the United Ministry to Evacuees in Chicago:

After the two relocation hostels were opened in Chicago, near the first of March, 1943, relocation of Japanese Americans to the city increased immensely. By the end of April, the number had grown to between one thousand and fifteen hundred. It was soon evident that this rapid influx would create certain social problems for the city. Chicago could not possibly absorb these people at the rate they were coming through the slow normal process of assimilation. There was common agreement that unless special efforts were begun at once, the Japanese Americans would follow the unfortunate pattern set by other racial minority groups, of creating their own economic and socially segregated community. Many old-time citizens pointed out that Chicago had enough racial minority problems of segregation, and they didn't want another. Most believed that because of the war, attention and criticism would soon be focused upon a Japanese "Little Tokyo." It was quite evident that to relocate a large group of people was one job, but to integrate them was another.

Believing that the Chicago Church Federation could greatly assist in the integration of the newcomers, Mr. Herman Will, then Midwest secretary of the F.O.R., and I presented our concern to Dr. John Harms and Mr. Virgil Lowder, of the Federation, about May 1, 1943.

Near the end of May, the Chicago Advisory Committee for Evacuees held a meeting. The integration program under contemplation by the Church Federation was presented for discussion and action. It was unanimously accepted as the will of the Committee. The Church Federation was requested and authorized to carry forward the integration program vigorously.

The carefully selected ministers were called together on June 4. The entire problem was set before them. A map indicating the distribution of resettlers by areas had been prepared as a means of visualizing the problem. The areas of resettler concentration were noted. All of those present were challenged to accept the responsibility of becoming minister-counselors to the resettlers, dedicating a portion of their time to calling upon them, counseling them in regard to religious, vocational, avocational, and personal problems. It was pointed out that those accepting such a responsibility would be considered as staff members of the United Ministry to Evacuees and charged with the task of integrating the newcomers into the normal social and religious life of the community.

Twenty of those present agreed to become members of the staff and voted to put the plan into effect. Each was given the names, addresses, and interests—religious and avocational—of the Nisei in his particular area of the city. In addition, each was given a prepared list of counseling suggestions and a list compiled by the Chicago Recreation Commission of the social and organizational resources in his particular neighborhood. It was agreed by the group that they should convene periodically to report their experiences, improve their counseling technique, and discuss future plans.

Near the beginning of June, several ministers of Japanese ancestry resettled in Chicago. It was thought wise to enlist the cooperation of these men in the integration program. After consultation with the ministers of Japanese ancestry, with various denominational leaders, and others, a plan was finally worked out whereby these ministerial newcomers would be supported financially by their respective denominations and join the staff of minister-counselors.

On June 23, the original staff of the Ministry to Evacuees, the ministers of Japanese ancestry, and representatives from various community agencies interested in integration met to hear reports of progress from the minister-counselors. From these reports, this ministry, one of the most forward-looking and unique interracial policies ever formulated in the history of Protestant America, seemed to be well under way.

At its June 28 meeting, this committee urged that the Church Federation's Department of Social Service continue to supervise the work of the ministry until a full time co-director could be secured to replace me. It also took steps to enlarge and reconstitute its membership in accordance with the recently adopted statement of policy.

Thereupon, the Reverend John Yamazaki and I, as co-directors, mailed to all resettlers letters of welcome. These letters invited resettlers to attend the churches and to call upon members of the United Ministry staff for counsel and help. The names and addresses of the minister-counselors were enclosed. Lists of new arrivals were obtained from the W.R.A., Brethren Relocation Hostel, and the American Friends Service Committee.

It became evident that most of the minister-counselors in their visits and counseling were going no further than attempting to associate resettlers with the churches. Realizing that complete integration into the normal community meant more than this, I decided to enlist the cooperation of three other agencies in our integration campaign, hoping that they could assist in the social and recreational aspects. Contacts were made with the Y.W.C.A., Y.M.C.A., and the Chicago Park District.

The Y.W.C.A. agreed to put a Nisei, Miss Kimi Mukaye, on their Chicago staff to organize a program for better integrating Nisei girls into Y.W.C.A. activities. Similar interest was shown by the Y.M.C.A., which asked us to submit a plan whereby it could use its existing staff and facilities for increasing Nisei participation in Y.M.C.A. activities.

The Chicago Park District greeted our suggestions and objective with real enthusiasm. They called a special meeting of the park supervisors from seventeen parks located in areas where Nisei were settling. These supervisors not only agreed to integrate Nisei who came to the park activities, but asked to know who the minister-counselors were in their particular areas. Some even asked for the names and addresses of resettlers so that they could visit them and invite them to park activities.

In July, Dr. Winburn T. Thomas of the Foreign Missions Conference temporarily took over my position and ably carried the work until September, when Mr. Roy Smith, formerly a missionary in Japan under the Methodist board, succeeded him. Mr. and Mrs. Howard D. Hannaford, missionaries under the Presbyterian board, U.S.A., who had returned on the *Gripsholm* and worked at Tule Lake relocation center, also joined the staff.

The Chicago United Ministry has accomplished a great deal, but there is no adequate means of determining the extent of its success. Mr. Smith mentions one great difficulty involved in this work:

Resettlers move about very frequently. In one area we had 430 names and addresses of resettlers. Upon checking these, we found that 122 had moved out of the area during the year, leaving 308. Fifty-two of the 308 letters that we sent out to them were returned marked "no longer here." Among the 256 remaining ones, we found that several more had moved from the area. This means that during one year, at least 41 per cent moved their place of living. It may be that this percentage is much higher, since many of the letters elicited no reply.

Besides Chicago, similar activities are carried on in other major areas of resettlement. Outstanding examples of individuals engaged in counseling are:

The Reverend Daisuke Kitagawa in Minneapolis, director, United Christian Ministry to Japanese Americans;

The Reverend Shigeo Tanabe, counselor, Detroit Council of Churches;

The Rev. Shunji Nishi (succeeded by the Reverend Donald Toriumi in September, 1945), field counselor, Cleveland Federation of Churches;

The Reverend John Yamasaki, Jr., counselor, Cincinnati Council of Churches.

Counseling services by these ministers of Japanese ancestry now form an essential part of the program of united ministry locally. They are also indispensable as interpreters and in paving the way for the evacuees.

Mr. Nishi reported in April, 1943, as follows:

We find that there is an *average* attendance *each Sunday* of some 156 to 160 Japanese Americans in 35 churches of various communions in Greater Cleveland. Of this number, 57 individuals have been received into membership (either by transfer or confession of faith) in 16 churches. The enrollment of children in church schools is also encouraging.

Out of this number we find 5 church school teachers, 4 singing in choirs, 3 leading Boy Scout activities, several participating in athletic activities. There is one Nisei serving in the triple capacity of choir member, church school teacher, and president of the Young People's Fellowship. A considerable number participate in various week day activities.

Another significant service being rendered by the Japanese American ministers is visitation to families now scattered about. In Colorado, Utah, Wyoming, Nebraska, and western Washington, such visitation to resettled families is greatly appreciated.

The Reverend Kojiro Unoura of the Disciples has done this extensively, and writes:

In such a situation as this the minister is always welcome, regardless of religious affiliation. This is especially true of those who have resettled from relocation centers or voluntarily evacuated from California. The other evening I was calling on such a family. The visit was extended far into the night as they poured out the experiences of their plight. I was up on my feet to bid them good-night, when the husband interrupted me by saying that there was still something else which meant so much to his family that he wished to tell me about it before I left. He said that where he had lived for over thirty long years, he and his family had never been able to make friends with his Caucasian neighbors. When they moved into this area they were met with friendliness and cordiality by the Caucasian neighbors. "Every member of my family," he said, "is remembered by our landlord on our birthdays with some gifts of kind remembrances to make us happy." He continued by saying that not only the landlord, but all the neighbors' children and young people came and visited with them so naturally and freely they now felt like human beings. He said, "Our children tell us that if we wish to leave after the war, it is perfectly all right with them, but they will stay right here where they can enjoy friendly relations with their neighbors."

"Mr. Unoura," he concluded, "after everything is said about

the bitter experiences of our evacuation, the whole ordeal was worth going through, if we can resettle in such a friendly neighborhood as this." Thus ended my visit. By the way, this family is Buddhist.[1]

In New York City, Denver, and Salt Lake City there are pre-war Japanese churches, with Japanese ministers serving Japanese congregations. In Cleveland, Chicago, and Minneapolis, Japanese groups have religious activities at Caucasian churches, apart from the program of united ministry. At Seabrook Farms, Bridgeton, New Jersey, a Japanese church is in process of formation.

Thus both the integration and the segregation (voluntary) patterns are developing across the country. Denominational heads of the boards of home missions, with the exception of one major denomination, have agreed as an ultimate ideal on the principle of integration, with a proviso that for Japanese-speaking members Issei ministers will be provided. This agreement includes an understanding that when the ideal of integration is impossible, an interdenominational approach will be made.

A few denominations are definitely committed to the policy of not starting Japanese churches again. The denomination that took exception to the forenamed agreement went ahead with the reopening of the former Japanese churches, not necessarily serving its former members exclusively, but with a definite probability of restoring the status of the pre-war days. It is as yet not clear whether other denominations can long adhere to the agreement in the face of this possibility. The whole future of missions to the

[1] From "The Christian Ministry in Exile," in *World Call,* a Disciples of Christ publication, November, 1944, p. 20.

Japanese, and, therefore, to other Orientals, remains in a delicate balance.

What the Christian leaders of Japanese ancestry think has equal, if not more, influence upon this matter. The Reverend Masahiko Wada, an Issei Baptist minister, says:

Though at present many of the Nisei [Christians] have been dispersed and have joined regular American churches, it is with reason feared that as the number of Nisei members in one place increases, it will create a problem for the churches as well as for the communities concerned.

In view of this fear, what the superintendent of a certain denomination [Methodist] has done in making a plan for separate churches for persons of Japanese ancestry seems to me an act of wisdom and foresight.

We must go along with the slow progress of the times and plan accordingly. If we take the importance of Issei churches too lightly and neglect to re-establish Japanese churches, we shall, by our default, allow the Buddhists to take advantage of the situation and make deep inroads into the life of the Japanese in America. We must, therefore, earnestly seek the best possible solution, with wise planning and prayer, so that the task of evangelism may not be neglected.

As for Nisei, the greatest problem is that of unchurched Japanese Americans. For their sake, more Nisei ministers should be trained. They should either be connected with American churches as ministers to Nisei, or work for the re-establishment of the former Japanese churches. I feel this to be of utmost urgency.

The Reverend James Sugioka, a Nisei minister of the Disciples of Christ, speaks for another view:

The paths of Christians of Japanese descent in America seem to have taken several directions toward the road of full Christian fellowship and abundant living.

There are those who advocate a completely segregated program for Christians of Japanese ancestry. But it seems to me that they are losing the meaning of true brotherhood and Christian unity. Christian ideals must become a reality in order to become effective.

The average young American of Japanese descent wants to be considered as an individual and to be accepted as any other American. Many have not yet achieved that goal. Christianity has led the way for many who have reached that goal and many more will need the same guidance. It means personal contact with those who know the way of Christ, both members of their own race as well as those of other races. The brave must lead the timid and those that see well must lead those of lesser vision.

For the members of the older generation who do not speak English, the gospel must be brought to them in the tongue they understand. This will mean a united effort by all denominations to minister to their particular needs.

A program of united effort interdenominationally for the dwindling few with language difficulty, and an aggressive approach to the already existing program of the various churches for the Japanese Americans, are two of the ways in which full integration can be assured.

We must not fall back into the rut of pre-evacuation days and call it a victory for the kingdom of God. There is a path through this present wilderness clear and bright. Let not those that have ideas and ideals other than those of Jesus Christ lead us astray.

Below is a poetic word of thanksgiving uttered by an Issei minister on the occasion of his departure from his parish at Poston relocation center. Whatever the future holds for Japanese Christians, a people in whom poetry has not perished will not lose the vision of God.

For us, Poston was a school of the desert. It was a school of love. A desert from time immemorial has been a testing ground. I imagine Jesus' experiences in the desert must have been like those in this desert. The journey for forty years of the Jews out of Egypt was also a journey of the desert.

A desert makes a man, trains a race, and brings them close to God. The blessing that Christians have received from their life in this desert for the last three years has not been small.[2]

[2] A letter from the Reverend T. Iwanaga, for many years an officer of the Salvation Army, since 1941 a minister of an independent Japanese church in Los Angeles.

8

From Camp to Campus

T HE story of student relocation is perhaps the happiest
of all the chapters on relocation. Behind it stood a
group of people who labored tirelessly with devotion, patience, and sacrifice.

The organization charged with the responsibility of student relocation was the National Japanese American Student Relocation Council, with headquarters in Philadelphia.
Its successive directors, Dean Robert O'Brien, Mr. Carlisle
V. Hibbard, Mrs. Helga Swan, Mrs. Elizabeth Emlen, and
Miss Ann Graybill, its most enthusiastic ex-field director,
Mr. Thomas Bodine, and other staff members, must feel a
great sense of satisfaction in having carried out a unique
enterprise of student relocation, an unprecedented event in
the student world of America, to an almost wholly successful conclusion. These excerpts from one of the Council's
own statements—prepared, of course, prior to the end of the
war—summarize its history and work:

In early May, 1942, the director of the War Relocation Authority addressed a letter to the executive secretary of the
American Friends Service Committee in Philadelphia, inviting
him to call together all the various groups at work on the
problem of student relocation and organize a national council
to carry out the program. The Assistant Secretary of War,
John J. McCloy, expressed his approval of the program: "Any-

thing that can legitimately be done to compensate loyal citizens of Japanese ancestry for the dislocation to which they have been subjected, by reason of military necessity, has our full approval."

Thus on May 29, 1942, in Chicago, the National Japanese American Student Relocation Council was born, with offices in Philadelphia, Seattle, Portland, Berkeley, and Los Angeles (all of which were later centralized in one office in Philadelphia). Its membership has included college presidents and deans, officers of college associations, representatives of leading Protestant churches, Jews, Catholics, Quakers, and the Student Y.M.C.A. and Y.W.C.A. Its costs of operation have been met by generous grants from the church boards and from two phil- anthropic foundations, one in New York and one in San Francisco.

In March of 1942, following the announcement of the govern- ment's plans for evacuating all persons of Japanese ancestry from the West Coast war zones, many college people up and down the coast became concerned about the twenty-five hundred young men and women of Japanese ancestry enrolled in colleges and universities in the military areas. Under the leadership of the Y.M.C.A., Y.W.C.A., the Pacific College Association, and such West Coast college presidents as Robert Gordon Sproul of the University of California, Lee Paul Gieg of the University of Washington, and Remsen Bird of Occidental College, groups of educators, students, and church people quickly formed to try to arrange for the immediate transfer of as many Nisei as possible to campuses east of the military areas. Letters were written to colleges and friends all over the country. Question- naires were sent out. Students were interviewed. To coordinate this activity, a Student Relocation Committee was organized in Berkeley on March 21, and met weekly during the months of April and May. An appropriation was secured from the National Y.M.C.A. and Y.W.C.A. and an executive secretary hired.

At its first meeting, the consensus of this West Coast committee was that evacuation was neither necessary nor expedient and that an appeal should be addressed to the authorities to alter its character from a wholesale removal of *all* persons of Japanese ancestry to a discriminating removal of potentially dangerous individuals. When this appeal failed, the committee began the work of determining which students would want to continue their education, what their needs were, and where in the East and Midwest they might go. In all, about seventy-five students found their way east in those first frantic days of March and April, 1942, before the National Student Relocation Council was organized.

As the months have gone by, the military regulations under which the Council has operated have become steadily more liberal. In the summer of 1942, the Council had difficulty securing from the Western Defense Command permission to enter the assembly centers for the purpose of distributing student relocation questionnaires and interviewing prospective students. In the early summer of 1942, the military authorities in Washington felt that for security reasons no evacuee student should attend any college within twenty-five miles of a railroad terminus. This decision seemed so restrictive that there was some question as to whether it was worth while to go forward with the program at all. Fortunately, it was modified later in the summer to provide that the names of colleges which had accepted an evacuee could be submitted to the War Department for clearance. Clearances came through slowly even for the smaller schools not engaged in war work. The program was handicapped by the delays involved and by the fact that a college had first to accept an evacuee before it could be determined whether the War Department would approve its enrolling such students.

In January of 1944, the military authorities lowered the restrictions further by announcing that henceforth clearance of institutions would not be necessary and that except for certain proscribed colleges and universities engaged in work important to the war effort, evacuees could attend on an ordinary W.R.A.

clearance the schools which accepted them; for attendance at the proscribed institutions, the student would be required to secure a special Provost Marshal General's clearance.

On August 21, 1944, the War Department removed all restrictions on the attendance of students of Japanese ancestry at educational institutions. The following telegram from the War Relocation Authority announced the change in policy: "Students to be accepted at all schools on same basis as any others." Finally, on December 17, 1944, the War Department announced that all persons of Japanese ancestry not individually excluded were free as of January 2, 1945, to return to the West Coast. With the complete lifting of the military restrictions, there is now no security reason for any college or university rejecting the application of a student of Japanese ancestry.

Most of the relocated students have earned a large part of their expenses through part-time employment. Many have worked before enrolling at school. Of the 3,000 relocated, only 741 have received grants through the Council. Some others have received aid direct from college, church, and other sources independently of the Council, but the large majority have financed their continued education through self-help and family resources. Up to December 31, 1944, a total of $188,972 in scholarship aid had been channeled through the Council, of which $140,361 came from thirteen national church boards, $34,971 from the World Student Service Fund, and $13,640 from other sources. A few of the church boards have set aside a certain percentage of their funds for grants to Buddhists and students who are not members of any church. The funds from the World Student Service Fund and various miscellaneous sources which the Council itself has had the responsibility of disbursing have been the principal source of help to students who are not members of a Christian church.

For some time prior to the lifting of the ban on the West Coast it had been possible for individuals to return, if they were able to secure special permission from the Western Defense Command. It was on one of these individual permits that Esther Takei, the first civilian student to return, reached Pasadena Junior College in September. Her arrival was heralded by press and radio up and down the West Coast. The professional "Jap" haters shouted their protests. But the good people of Pasadena quietly accepted her, and the storm passed by. When the Council's field director visited Esther in December, he reported that she was as happy as any student he knew in the East or Midwest, having experienced no personal hostility or discrimination, but only friendliness and fair play.

The Student Relocation Council not only pioneered in relocation but also assisted vigorously in the general relocation program by sending back to the camps during summer months Nisei students to interpret the "outside" to the residents. Church boards supported this project by providing "returnee" students' expenses.

Most of the evacuated students have successfully relocated. But the Council was also concerned with the graduates of the camp high schools who would ordinarily go on to college. Families interested in giving them advanced education had no private funds. Residents of the camps raised money to help worthy students, but out of meager earnings of an average of sixteen dollars a month, the most they could raise helped only a few.

After the closing of the camps, the families needed all the money they earned for the bare necessities of life. Unless outside help was forthcoming, Japanese Americans would either have to drop out of school if they were on a campus, or, if they had just graduated from a relocation center high school, give up hope of going to college.

The Council staff was concerned with them not because they were Nisei; their concern was for the difficult years facing these young people. Japanese Americans needed all
9

the preparation they could obtain at college. Those who worked with Japanese Americans discovered that the high average educational standard of the Nisei was one of the most important sources of stability and intelligent facing of their own problems.

"Intelligent leadership among Japanese Americans is unique among America's minorities. It saved Nisei from going astray; it saved America from a potential disaster in connection with the evacuation. Thank God for Nisei leadership."

These are the words of Dr. W. W. Alexander of the Rosenwald Foundation, uttered at the annual meeting of the Home Missions Council, at Atlantic City, N. J., in January, 1945.

The Student Relocation Council desired to preserve this leadership by sending a normal percentage of high school graduates to college. Since most of the boys had gone to the Army from the campuses, the need of providing higher education for those who could enroll seemed very important to the Council staff.

To many people, education at the higher level seems to be an occupation of a privileged class; in other words, luxury. But this war has demonstrated that those soldiers who knew how to think for themselves have served themselves and their comrades-in-arms better than those who knew only a certain thing to do in a given situation.

What the future holds for Japanese Americans, only God knows. But if we help train them to think for themselves, we may harvest incalculable benefit to the ultimate solution of our so-called "Japanese problem" in America.

9

Unfinished Business

THE church is concerned with the future of the Japanese Americans, whether Christians or not. It is not only aware of a unique opportunity to render a "Good Samaritan" service, but also of its obligation to a segment representing only one-tenth of one per cent of our total population. At times, the church's attention to them has seemed, to some people, disproportionately great. But in the face of the need of these people and in view of the stake both democracy and Christianity have therein, what the churches have done is no greater than the challenge that the problem has presented.

What is going to become of these people, and what are the churches expected to do from now on? Now that the relocation centers have been closed, can we not turn our attention to something else? The churches' relief program overseas has a large claim upon America's Christians. Churches must be prepared to meet the needs of returning veterans. The church ought to solve the race problem. It must counteract the growing secularism and materialism of our generation. The church's task never seems to end; it will never end if the church wants to be the church—not until the Kingdom comes.

In order to bring the world nearer to the Kingdom, we must act as Christians wherever we see a need. Among

130,000 persons of Japanese ancestry in our midst, there is still a large volume of unfinished business for the church. It is important at this juncture in our country's history and in the history of the church's relationship to them, that we see the need clearly and take appropriate action. "Justice delayed is justice denied." We cannot leave our task with respect to the Japanese Americans unfinished.

Let us, therefore, briefly review what the government has done since the establishment of the relocation centers and has announced it will do, in order to see our relationship to the whole problem in terms of our future task.

At the beginning of 1943, Congress directed an investigation of the relocation centers to determine whether or not the administration of the War Relocation Authority was at fault, as alleged by some critics of the agency after two minor disturbances within the centers. The investigating committee (a subcommittee of the Senate Military Affairs Committee, headed by Senator Chandler of Kentucky) recommended as a result of the investigation that a thoroughgoing individual "screening" be conducted with a view towards segregating the disloyal from the loyal.

On January 28, 1943, the War Department announced that the ranks of the Army would be opened to Japanese Americans who would volunteer for combat service. Since Pearl Harbor, citizens of Japanese ancestry had been denied an opportunity to serve their country in the armed forces, though more than 5,000 who were already in the Army before December 7, 1941, were not affected. Both in Hawaii and on the mainland of the United States, eager Nisei responded in large numbers to this new policy, going beyond the Army's quota of 2,500 to 10,000 in Hawaii, though in the relocation centers the response was not great enough to fill the quota.

It is an indisputable fact that while Nisei both in Hawaii and in the relocation centers had written the President and the War Department asking for this opportunity, enthusiasm in Hawaii was greater, mainly because the Japanese Americans in the Islands were not evacuated. Out of the former National Guard members of Hawaii was formed the 100th Infantry Battalion, which was transferred to Camp McCoy, Wisconsin, then to Camp Shelby, Mississippi, for intensive combat training.

In August, 1943, the battalion went to North Africa, and in the subsequent invasions of Sicily and Italy distinguished itself for courage and heroism under fierce enemy fire. It became one of the most decorated units in the United States Army, and was nicknamed the "Purple Heart Battalion." Nisei soldiers from the relocation centers and elsewhere in the United States joined it in later engagements in Italy and France, forming the 442nd Combat Team, need for replacement having been especially heavy among the Hawaiian volunteers. Many volunteers from the relocation centers also suffered death and injuries. When the fighting was particularly fierce, many parents in the centers received telegrams from the War Department reporting their sons' supreme sacrifice for the United States.

In an attempt to determine individual evacuees' loyalty to the United States, during the summer and fall of 1943, every resident, seventeen years or older, in the centers was given a questionnaire by the government. But the wording of some questions was such that the questionnaire caused great confusion and resentment among the residents, particularly the Issei. They were asked, among other things, if they would, in effect, renounce their Japanese nationality, without being given any assurance that their alien status under our present immigration laws would be changed. To this a large number of the aliens found it impossible to answer satisfactorily. Their sense of insecurity was further deepened. The government withdrew the first questionnaire and distributed a second, asking this time if Issei would abide by the laws of the United States and refrain from any act detrimental to the nation's war effort. As for the citizens, the questionnaire inquired if they would renounce any allegiance to any foreign government, or emperor, and pledge unqualified allegiance to the United States. For Americans of unhesitating loyalty any reference to a supposedly divided loyalty was felt to be an insult. Nevertheless, loyal Nisei answered in the affirmative without reservations.

Based upon the replies to the questionnaire and other information secured by the Federal agencies interested, individual hearings were conducted in the centers, and the process of segregation got under way in the fall. A total of 18,000 people have since been segregated at Tule Lake relocation center. Though this number includes those who definitely preferred to identify themselves and their future with Japan, the majority were those who did not feel they could continue the struggle in the United States and merely wished to spend the rest of their lives in the country of their birth. Also included were a large number of minors who were not asked to fill out a questionnaire but were members of the families whose heads were segregated.

It is significant that the overwhelming majority of both

the aliens and citizens expressed a preference to identify
themselves with the United States while still in the relocation centers.

On January 20, 1944, the War Department, impressed by
the outstanding record of the volunteers of Japanese ancestry in Italy, restored selective service to the Japanese Americans, thus removing as far as the War Department was concerned the last stigma of suspicion. War Department figures show that there were 22,532 Japanese Americans in
the Army in June, 1945.

When the War Relocation Authority was transferred to
the Department of the Interior in February, 1944, Secretary
Ickes made a statement that expressed eloquently the concern of the government. He said:

In carrying out my responsibilities under the order [an
executive order effecting the transfer], I intend to keep in mind
the need of recognition of the rights of the United States
citizens regardless of ancestry, the internal security of the United
States during wartime and the international implications which
are involved, and particularly the effect of this program on the
treatment of war prisoners and civilians in Japanese hands.

In the same month the first center, the Jerome relocation
center, Arkansas, was closed for good.

Meanwhile, the military situation in the Pacific steadily
improved for the United States. Danger to the West Coast
seemed eliminated. Remembering the words of President
Roosevelt that "we shall restore to the loyal evacuees the
right to return to the evacuated areas as soon as the military situation will make such restoration feasible," friendly
organizations and individuals, including most of the Protestant denominations, petitioned the government to remove

restrictions imposed upon loyal citizens and law-abiding aliens of Japanese ancestry. Proponents of the demand that all Japanese be not only kept out of the West Coast states but be sent back to Japan also raised their voices, reminiscent of the days before the mass evacuation.

On December 17, 1944, General H. C. Pratt, commanding general of the Western Defense Command, announced that effective January 2, 1945, the evacuation orders would be rescinded, as of that date, and the Secretary of War, Mr. Stimson, made the following statement to the nation:

The War Department is aware that the rescission of mass exclusion will create certain adjustment problems beyond military considerations. It believes, however, that adequate solutions for these problems exist. The Department of the Interior informed the War Department that it intends to put into effect a program based upon a gradual and orderly return to the West Coast and a vigorous continuation of its efforts to relocate persons of Japanese descent throughout the United States.

Mr. Ickes, as head of the department responsible for execution of this policy, reminded the people of America of a wider implication. He said:

It is the responsibility of every American worthy of citizenship in this great nation to do everything that he can to make easier the return to normal life of these people who have been cleared by the Army authorities. By our conduct towards them we will be judged by all the people of the world.

Following the rescission order of the Army, the Supreme Court of the United States had declared on December 18, 1944, that a loyal citizen cannot be held without due process of law, and thus all citizens of Japanese ancestry became legally free, as free as any other person, and Japanese aliens were placed on the same basis as other enemy aliens. The Army, however, retained the right to exclude anyone, citizen or alien, from certain areas. But this time it was on an individual basis.

That this rescission did not bring about an immediate mass return of the former residents of the West Coast or a friendly reception to those that did return in some regions is well known to us all. One spot that received nation-wide publicity for its hostility towards Japanese Americans was Hood River, Oregon. There the local American Legion Post removed (though it restored them later) the names of sixteen soldiers of Japanese ancestry from the Legion's Honor Roll, and warned Hood River's former residents not to come back. Incidents of vandalism occurred in Merced, Fresno, Auburn, and Livingston, California. Acts of terrorism including shooting, burning, and dynamiting were committed in an attempt to scare the Japanese Americans away. Arrests of culprits were made, but none was punished on any of the charges brought, up to June, 1945. A defense attorney in one of the cases pleaded, "This is a white man's country." Twenty-four such cases of terrorism had taken place when Secretary Ickes spoke out in indignation. On May 13, 1945, he said:

The shameful spectacle of these incidents of terrorism taking place at the back door of the San Francisco Conference, now in session to develop means by which men of all races can live together in peace, must end once and for all. I believe that an aroused national opinion rooted in the indignation of fair-minded Americans throughout the country will be a powerful aid to the West Coast states and local officers charged with bringing the vigilante criminals to justice.

Church organizations and citizens' fair-play committees, in cooperation with government agencies, were bending all their efforts to create a reasonable atmosphere for the return of the evacuees. In Hood River, the County Ministerial Association made its stand publicly clear when it declared:

We are agreed that if any service man is willing to suffer and die for the principles of the United States, he is worthy of having his name on any service honor roll and to have unlimited freedom to live among us. We consider it unjust, un-American, and unchristian to deprive them of their privileges and rights. It can only make more difficult the solution of racial problems and bring trouble and shame upon Hood River Valley.

The national commander of the American Legion advised the Hood River Post to reconsider its action, and the post complied with the advice. In the meantime, one of the sixteen Nisei gave his life on Leyte for the United States.

Schools in the relocation centers were closed at the end of the spring term in 1945. All other community activities along with internal employment were placed on a descending scale. The relocation of families, with the aged and small children, was admittedly difficult, involving real hardships in many cases. As of June 30, 1945, only 49,125, less than one-half, had left the centers, leaving 45,249 to be relocated, excluding the 17,454 at Tule Lake. Disagreement with the W.R.A. on the policy of closing all the centers before the end of the war, from a standpoint of genuine humanitarianism, was expressed by some. They were aware that many of the remaining families had little ability to make a living outside or had sent their sole breadwinners into the Army. The member denominations of the Committee on Resettlement of Japanese Americans, meeting in March, 1945, when the Committee was made a division of the Home Missions Council, agreed that even under the best of conditions the life in the relocation centers was abnormal and should not be continued any longer than necessary.

This agreement reflected the heavy responsibility upon the churches. Most Japanese church buildings were opened to serve as hostels. The Seattle Council of Churches, the Los Angeles Federation of Churches, the Southern California Federation of Churches, the Friends of the American Way, the Committee for American Principles and Fair Play, the Protestant Church Commission, the Federal Council of Churches, and many other religious bodies, including the Y.M.C.A., Y.W.C.A., and local councils of churches not mentioned above, were actively engaged in paving the way for the return. Federal, state, and local agencies improved their methods to cope with difficult situations, and the general conditions improved correspondingly. The W.R.A. worked hard. Though many of its defects in operation were criticized, it deserved the whole-hearted support of the people, particularly of Christians.

The need for intensified efforts was not confined to the Pacific Coast area, where tension was greatest. The churches' work in the rest of the country was equally important. In June, 1945, the Home Missions Council called several local and regional conferences of resettlement workers and representatives of interested groups for the purpose of discovering areas and types of needs. Delegates from these conferences gathered in New York, and from New York went to Washington, D. C., to give their views to the War Relocation Authority and the Department of the Interior.

A request was made to Secretary Ickes based upon the announced policy of the W.R.A. to close all field offices of the agency at the end of March, 1946. In behalf of the above-mentioned conferences, the delegation requested the Secretary to extend the life of the field operation of the W.R.A. "several months beyond 1945" in order to handle emergency problems faced by resettlers and returning Nisei service men and women. Mr. Ickes expressed the opinion that churches should be able to do even more than they had been doing to promote satisfactory resettlement.

Thus early in June, 1945, when the schools in the centers had just closed and before the mass movement of entire families coastward—which was later to grow by leaps and bounds—had begun to take form, resettlement committees east of the Rockies visualized the ongoing tasks as follows: In some places a trickle, in others a steady stream, of resettlers eastward could be expected until the end, most of them following others to the better known places of relocation. They were free to go, looking for jobs and homes. Prime responsibility for finding them permanent employment and homes and, in cases of need, for introducing them to regular welfare and emergency relief agencies, public and private, would be borne by the nearest W.R.A. offices. Local committees on resettlement would help, chiefly with cases specifically brought to their attention, and would assist in finding and providing temporary housing, including the hostel type. The local resettlement committees would be organized with the purpose of utilizing all possible community resources of personnel. They would include in their membership not only representatives of the churches, but also, where available, representatives of the Federal Public Housing

Authority, the local veterans' administration, persons skilled in the problems of labor and management, and experts in community service.

They would keep before them the goal of complete integration of the evacuees into the community life. Newcomers with church connections and preferences would be made to feel at home in churches near by. Children would be helped to find Sunday schools, as well as Boy and Girl Scouts and 4-H clubs and just playmates. School principals would be interviewed in advance when children of school age were coming. Parents would find their place in Parent-Teacher Associations; participation in community projects, such as the Y.M.C.A. and Y.W.C.A., Red Cross work, and War Fund drives, would be encouraged. If cases of discrimination or prejudice toward the newcomers developed, the committee would busy itself with an attempt to remove such prejudice.

As the task of complete integration might occupy a very long time, the committees would cooperate with other local agencies interested in preparation for carrying on the program of integration after the W.R.A. should close its work.

The same kind of forward looking would evidence itself in such projects as the raising of scholarship funds for vocational education of persons wishing to improve employment status.

Across the country on the West Coast it was felt that comparable committees could and would be established, although it was recognized that circumstances were much different.

Since the meeting in New York in June the War Relocation Authority announced an accelerated program of closing the relocation centers, fixing the dates of closing as follows:

October 1, 1945:	Units II and III of Poston, Arizona
	Canal Unit, Gila, Arizona
October 15, 1945:	Granada, Colorado
November 1, 1945:	Topaz, Utah
	Minidoka, Idaho
November 15, 1945:	Heart Mountain, Wyoming
	Butte Unit, Gila, Arizona
December 1, 1945:	Unit I of Poston, Arizona
	Manzanar, California
December 15, 1945:	Rohwer, Arkansas

A directive was issued by the W.R.A. requiring all residents to make their relocation plans six weeks prior to the date of the closing of the camp in which they resided. If the evacuees were unable to make their own plans, plans would be made for them by the W.R.A. If they chose no place to which to go, they were to be sent back to the place of their pre-evacuation residence. If they were not able to support themselves, assistance was to be arranged for them.

In this scheme of the W.R.A. there was a great deal to be praised. All church folk and other fair-minded people heartily endorsed the fundamental principle of restoring normal life to the dislocated. But as the exodus from the camps was accelerated, hardships ensued on a large scale. Hostels were overcrowded, and finding suitable housing was extremely difficult.

Government housing made available was at best an emergency set-up offering little permanency or normalcy. Mass relocation, such as the one to Seabrook Farms, New Jersey, where more than seventeen hundred evacuees were relocated in October, 1945, living in a camp-like atmosphere, was not a long-time solution.

The aged, sick, and infirm among the Issei faced with the

greatest of hesitation the necessity of accepting public relief assistance because procedures were cumbersome and embarrassing.

People all over the country who had loyally supported the W.R.A. program of relocation were deeply disturbed over the turn the program took. Back in 1942 they were opposed to the wholesale evacuation of one group of people on the basis of racial ancestry. They demanded a more discriminating policy than the forcible segregation of the entire Japanese population. They urged resettlement. They helped the W.R.A. and the evacuees in realizing it. In doing all these things, they were motivated by a sense of democratic responsibility and humane concern for the people who were victimized. Their anxiety in 1945 was based on the same principle—a Christian and democratic treatment of the evacuees. They were disturbed because the manner in which the evacuees were coming out suggested the use of undue pressure by the W.R.A. in the centers. Some pressure might have been necessary to "pump life" into the evacuees who had lost their initiative, but when after being pressed to go out, they were unable to find a place to live, the mere moving out did not seem to harmonize with the best interests of society or the welfare of the evacuees. It was to be expected, therefore, that when indigent persons were returned to a community tension would grow. Acceptance by the public of self-supporting and progressive Nisei was one thing. Absorbing dependent and aged Issei, unfortunately, was quite another.

It was clear that a whole group of people literally uprooted from their homes and jobs, confined in custody for military reasons, could not be restored to their former status after more than three years of absence. They were not returned into a vacuum created by the evacuation. They came back into a packed community, their former places of residence and business mostly occupied, into an area of our country where economic, political, and social tension was more critical than before the war, with more racial and ethnic problems to be solved than when "the Japanese problem" was the main issue. The presence of other racial minority groups seemed on the surface to divide the attention of the race baiters, but actually it aggravated the general race tension. When minority groups supplied sorely needed manpower, there was tolerance. It was felt in the fall of 1945 that if the industrial capacity of the West Coast should fail to meet all employment needs, a serious situation could arise.

Individuals and organizations that helped in preparing the West Coast for the return of the evacuees became frankly apprehensive lest the drastic policy of the W.R.A. increase strain both on the communities and on the evacuees. Many of those individuals and organizations suggested alternatives to the government. The Protestant Church Commission for Japanese Service at its executive committee meeting on August 1, 1945, adopted one such resolution. It was in essence as follows:

Guaranteed housing should precede an evacuee family's return or relocation. If this is impossible, an *interim center* close to the evacuees' point of origin should be provided.

A special *Federal assistance fund* should be set up to provide for *aged persons* who cannot qualify for categorical aid in their respective states because of alien status, and for other *persons incapable of self-support*. Pending the establishment of such a

Federal assistance program, one relocation center should be kept open as a *maintenance center* for such people.

Japanese American troops should be assured, because of their long and essential service overseas, that their dependents and immediate families will not suffer disproportionate hardships, such as will result by default of this program. (All italics theirs.)

The Commission added this important footnote to the foregoing resolutions:

The interests of the nation, as well as the evacuees themselves, require that they become independent elements in the life of their communities, except those permanently impoverished by the original evacuation; and

The United States cannot jeopardize its international moral leadership by ill-considered treatment of its own citizens and people dislocated by war.

The Federal Council of Churches at its executive meeting on September 18, 1945, urged the Secretary of the Interior that the government provide *adequate* provision for the returning evacuees. Likewise, the Home Missions Council through its Resettlement Division, meeting on October 3, 1945, called upon the government to do everything possible to meet the needs of the evacuees who were returning.

To render counseling services to the families that stayed to the very end, the Committee on Resettlement arranged to send interpreters to the centers. Thus through October and November, 1945, Mr. Jobu Yasumura (Baptist), Mr. Masao Satow (Y.M.C.A.), and Mr. Sam Ishikawa (Friends Service) visited four camps.

On November 8, the Home Missions Council sponsored in New York a National Conference on Japanese Americans, to discuss immediate and future problems Japanese Ameri-

10

cans were facing. As an indication of widespread interest in the subject, forty national private social welfare and religious groups sent sixty-nine delegates for a full day's deliberations. Mrs. Ruth W. Kingman, executive secretary of the Pacific Coast Committee on American Principles and Fair Play, came specially to report on the conditions on the West Coast.

As the result of the conference, a letter was sent to President Harry S. Truman. The three major points requested of the President were as follows:

1. That you authorize by executive order the creation of a temporary agency within the Department of the Interior to continue while necessary Federal services to the evacuees after the War Relocation Authority goes out of existence next June. Our experience has shown that the several Federal departments concerned with housing, social security, and employment require coordination of their work in relation to this particular minority, whose problems are distinct and for whom the government has a peculiar responsibility, since the problems were created by the evacuation.

2. That you recommend to the Congress procedure for the consideration of the legitimate indemnity claims of this minority, whose property losses as a result of the forced evacuation were enormous. They were obliged to sell property at a fraction of its value or lease or rent it at nominal figures. Confusion reigned under the pressure of the Army's orders for speedy internment and many lost land, buildings, and movable goods altogether. Since this was a war measure, it is clearly the responsibility of the Federal government to make proper restitution. These war claims certainly have as strong a moral justification as others recognized by the government. But there is no way of meeting them without Congressional appropriations out of which the Federal courts may meet what they find to be legitimate charges against the government.

3. That the Department of Justice be requested to adopt a fair and humane policy in the deportation of interned Japanese aliens and those who renounced their citizenship. Consideration should be given to the fact that many of the aliens have American-born children, some of whom have served honorably in our armed forces. Such families should not be broken up. All alien Japanese residents who desire to remain in the United States and concerning whom there is no convincing record of disloyalty should be given hearings, if necessary.

The letter to the President was answered promptly, though not by Mr. Truman himself. On December 18, 1945, the Department of Justice wrote to the Home Missions Council on the question of the deportation as follows:

No Japanese alien or renunciant American citizen of Japanese ancestry will be repatriated against his will unless he is found to be repatriable under standards which have been established for German alien enemies. This determination will in most cases be made through a hearing procedure, and the standards adopted permit taking into account mitigating circumstances such as hardship to close relatives and the like.

Mr. Dillon S. Myer, director of W.R.A., expressed his views on the matters of continued government responsibility and indemnification. He said:

To establish a new Federal agency at that time [June 30, 1946, when W.R.A. goes out of existence] exclusively for the evacuees would, I believe, tend to perpetuate the segregation of these people and might even encourage the racist forces to push for further discriminatory measures.

I fully agree that some procedure should be established so that evacuees can present claims to a special board or commission for losses or damages actually suffered as a result of the evacuation. We are planning to make recommendations on this subject, through the Secretary of the Interior, in the very near future.

In the meantime, all relocation centers were closed, some of them more than two weeks ahead of schedule. On December 1, 1945, there was only Tule Lake center in northern California open.

At Tule Lake, a procedure had been in operation since the end of the hostilities whereby those eligible for relocation were given clearance, and others were either transferred to internment camps or deported to Japan. Up to the end of February, 1946, nearly seven thousand individuals sailed for Japan, the majority of them repatriating according to their wishes, and others, members of the families, accompanying the heads of the families with consent. It was quite possible that among them were quite a few who went to Japan reluctantly.

The people at Tule Lake lived through a tragic period in a tragic way. To say that they invited their plight hardly described the problem of many of them. Their tragedy was a human situation—the consequence of circumstances and human nature. For how else would an old man past seventy hang himself in his lonely barrack? How else would a mother go insane, torn between her loyalty to her husband who chose to go to Japan and her love for her two children who were determined to remain in America?

Throughout the last days of Tule Lake, a few faithful ministers and missionaries remained with the people. Perhaps the problem that the majority of the residents of that unhappy camp faced was beyond the scope of the church's ministry. But the *unbroken* continuity of services is a record of which only the church can boast. Only, the church would not boast, for its own representatives in Tule Lake felt the inadequacy and helplessness of the token attention they received from the "outside" during the last period. These few co-workers with God had to make their own presence count as fully as possible. Thus, when one of the ministers voluntarily repatriated with a group of several hundreds bound for Japan, in December, 1945, his presence was a manifestation of true shepherdhood. And to the missionaries who remained to the last, the church owed a real debt, though they would not expect any special recognition for services rendered for Christ.

Where are the rest of the evacuees now, who in 1942 totaled 106,775? According to the W.R.A. report of January 31, 1946, the three West Coast states received 49,517, or 47 per cent. In the remainder of the country, the states claiming a large number are, in the order of evacuee population: Washington, Illinois, Utah, Colorado, Oregon, Idaho, Ohio, New York, and New Jersey. Those who stayed where they had relocated made satisfactory readjustment on the whole. Many difficult personal problems required much patience and fortitude on their part, but they remained the same self-disciplining people in the period of transition and adjustment that they had proved to be during the drastic and hectic days of mass evacuation.

Economically, there are not today as many independent industries or businesses operated by persons of Japanese descent as in pre-war days, but the process of self-support through employment is well under way, though there is yet much to be desired in fair employment practices, especially on the West Coast.

As for their social integration, it is a slow process, and no scientific measurement can be applied to gauge its success. Too much pressure for "integration" has done some harm in some cases, making individuals overly self-conscious. The majority are living like any normal human being, seeking company with those of similar interest and congeniality. Most notable among those who found kindred souls in non-Japanese groups are the Nisei in professions, labor unions, and religious organizations.

In the world of labor, CIO's positive policy and practice of non-discrimination are matched by the unfailing adherence to it of new Nisei members. The church has much to learn from labor unions in the matter of race relations, and the Nisei, like many others of racial and religious minority groups, have today a keener sense of criticism and appreciation based upon the performance rather than the slogan of those who approach them.

Thanks to the painful experiences in race relations during the war, the larger community is now more conscious of its responsibility to its different smaller ethnic communities within itself. As regards Japanese Americans, several midwestern and eastern cities have now acquired sufficient knowledge of and experience with the general problem of persons of Japanese ancestry to deal with it through existing agencies of social services.

On the Pacific Coast, the focal point of the evacuation controversy, communities are organizing for civic unity. Made conscious of their responsibility by the evacuation and being desirous of curing causes of interracial tension, California has now become the first state in the Union to have a State Council of Civic Unity, coordinating the work of a hundred and twenty-four local civic unity and fair-play groups. The membership in these groups is splendidly representative of all kinds of people: liberals and "reactionaries," church people and non-church people, workers and industrialists, and Negroes, Mexicans, Orientals, and Caucasians.

What happened on the Pacific Coast in 1942 could not have but taught the country a great lesson. Whether all legal experts agree with him or not, Professor Eugene V. Rostow of Yale Law School stated in an article entitled "Our Worst Wartime Mistake" *(Harpar's Magazine,* September, 1945):

The Japanese exclusion program rests on five propositions of the utmost potential menace:

1. Protective custody, extending over three or four years, is a permitted form of imprisonment in the United States.

2. Political opinions, not criminal acts, may contain enough danger to justify such imprisonment.

3. Men, women, and children of a given racial group, both Americans and resident aliens, can be presumed to possess the kind of dangerous ideas which require their imprisonment.

4. In time of war or emergency the military—perhaps without even the concurrence of the legislature—can decide what political opinions require imprisonment, and which groups are infected with them.

5. The decision of the military can be carried out without indictment, trial, examination, jury, the confrontation of witnesses, counsel for the defense, or any of the other safeguards of the Bill of Rights.

These words of Professor Rostow require serious pondering. It is possible—nay, it is hoped with the strongest of hopes—that no such evacuation ever be repeated.

With the civic unity organizations throughout the Pacific Coast, and both the American Council on Race Relations and the American Civil Liberties Union, each with West Coast branch offices, actively striving for better community interracial relations and civil liberties protection, we may express our social and legal concern through these agencies.

What remains for the churches? Before answering the question, let us note the status of each of the three major national agencies that represented the churches' interest in Japanese Americans.

The Protestant Church Commission for Japanese Service, which served in the relocation centers and assisted the returned evacuees on the West Coast, became independent of the Home Missions Council of North America during 1945, and continued its functions of coordination and services.

The Committee on Resettlement of Japanese Americans terminated its services with the liquidation of the relocation centers, at the end of 1945. The Administrative Committee for Japanese Work of the Home Missions Council, which had supervised the Committee on Resettlement, carried on a limited service until April, 1946, and thereafter remained in readiness to meet any new problem that might arise, but otherwise returned to its normal duties of administrative activities relative to home missions work among Japanese. Questions of social action and race relations involving the churches' responsibility to Japanese Americans are the concern of the two regular departments of the Federal Council of Churches specifically charged with such matters. The emphasis is on using the "ongoing" and local agencies of the church wherever and whenever the need is recognized.

The National Japanese American Student Relocation Council decided in February, 1946, to close its office on April 30, the same year. Four thousand Nisei students and graduates remember the Council with grateful hearts.

That these national agencies specially created to solve the

Japanese American problem transferred their functions to the ongoing agencies and local groups did indicate the passing of emergency, but not the end of the problem. In the real sense, the problem has now been integrated into the general and pressing problem of race relations in the country, requiring Christian social action.

Japanese Americans are interested in, as others of racial and religious minorities are, and the churches are in favor of (1) Fair Employment Practice law, (2) minimum wage law, (3) full employment law, (4) housing act, (5) repeal of anti-alien land law (in several states), (6) removal of discrimination in the immigration laws, (7) international cooperation through the United Nations Organization and guaranty of individual liberty everywhere. To these objectives the church people of America can give their support.

Legislation is essential, but education is basic. During 1946 the churches are making a special study of race relations. Knowledge of facts will eliminate much of the still existing prejudice towards Japanese Americans. But books and lectures can hardly remove all prejudice. The best education for better race relations is personal contact. Let us seek our own freedom from prejudice by making friends with individuals of a racial stock other than our own. Making an exhibit of a person from another racial group at a church meeting and calling it a race relations program is not recommended. Paternalistic treatment must be avoided. Enter into a genuine fellowship, and you will forget that you are promoting better race relations.

The most crucial problem in the church is that of the place of the leadership of the minority groups. For the church and Japanese Americans, it is the future of Nisei pastors.

Unless the Nisei pastor finds a real place in the life of the entire church for his leadership and service, the tendency for perpetual segregation in the church can never be expected to dissolve itself. On this vital question, Mr. Jobu Yasumura, a well known Christian leader, expresses the following personal opinion that is worth our utmost consideration:

A sizable number of Nisei young men are now studying for the ministry. While their fellow students receive a call to a church by the time they are in their final term, the average Nisei theological students can hope only at best to secure an assistant pastorate ministering to other Nisei. There is today only one Nisei pastor, the Reverend Jitsuo Morikawa, who ministers, along with a Caucasian co-pastor, to a predominantly Caucasian church. Most churches needing pastors would pass up qualified Nisei pastors or actually turn down Nisei candidates. A number of churches have accepted Nisei members into their membership. This is fine, but one wonders if integration would be accepted on the upper levels of ministerial positions as well as acceptance on the level of membership.

This is not so much an indictment of the church as it is a plea for understanding of what the Nisei students of theology are up against. This is also a plea to Nisei students of theology to realize what they are up against if they expect to become pastors of Caucasian churches. It may not be impossible, but the Nisei must be better trained, better qualified, and so far superior to the average candidate that color becomes a minor factor. . . .

All this places a serious responsibility on denominational educational boards that will continue to help Nisei students. Already some denominations have withdrawn special tuition scholarships to Nisei students altogether, except to those who will go into religious training in their own denominational schools or seminaries. Some Nisei have, as a result, changed their field of studies from secular to religious, just to be able to continue their schooling. Unless these denominations are prepared to place these Nisei

Christian workers and ministers in centers and churches on the basis of their qualifications it is short of criminal to lure sincere young people into the sacrificial sanctifications of a Christian life of service.

Stated positively, we need more Nisei Christian leaders who have better than average training and ability, fired by an imagination and forcefulness to answer any questions about their fitness for Christian service. We need enlightened Christian bodies that will not recede when faced by reactionary forces that plead for expediency in interracial relations. We need Christian leaders and churches that not only believe in the brotherhood of man as a principle but as the basis for an active program of action that actually brings peoples of all minorities into continuing fellowship at all levels of contacts.

This and other blueprints for action are not for organized groups only. In the final analysis what the church does is what local churches do, and what a local church does is what each individual member does. The unfinished part of our business, as regards Japanese Americans, then, is what remains to be done: to render out of date any reference to a group of people as "Japanese Americans." It is the same kind of business that the church has everywhere in the United States and, for that matter, throughout the world—making real the divine plan of God, the unity of the human race.

Appendix

I

A: COMMITTEE ON RESETTLEMENT OF JAPANESE AMERICANS
(October, 1942-March, 1945)

Sponsored Jointly by

The Federal Council of the Churches of Christ in America
The Home Missions Council of North America

in cooperation with

The Foreign Missions Conference of North America

THE CONSTITUENT BODIES AND EXECUTIVE COMMITTEE

Church of the Brethren, Congregational and Christian Churches, Disciples of Christ, Evangelical Church, Evangelical and Reformed Church, Friends, Mennonites, Methodist Church, Northern Baptist Convention, Presbyterian Church in the U. S. A., Protestant Episcopal Church, Reformed Church in America, United Brethren Church, United Presbyterian Church.

THE COOPERATING BODIES

Family Welfare League of America, National Board of Young Women's Christian Associations, National Council of Young Men's Christian Associations.

THE EXECUTIVE COMMITTEE

Hermann N. Morse, *chairman;* J. Quinter Miller, *secretary-treasurer;* Roswell P. Barnes, Mark A. Dawber, John W. Thomas.

THE STAFF

George E. Rundquist, *executive secretary;* Toru Matsumoto, *assistant;* Willis G. Hoekje, *assistant.*

B: COMMITTEE ON RESETTLEMENT OF JAPANESE AMERICANS
(March, 1945-December, 1945)

Operated as Resettlement Division under the Committee on the Administration of Japanese Work of the Home Missions Council. George A. Wieland, *chairman;* Mark A. Dawber, *executive secretary.*

THE CONSTITUENT BODIES AND COOPTED MEMBERS
(Coopted members marked by *)

Church of the Brethren, Church of God, Colored Methodist Episcopal, Congregational and Christian Churches, Disciples of Christ, Evangelical and Reformed Church, Friends, Methodist Church, Northern Baptist Convention, Presbyterian Church in the U. S. A., Protestant Episcopal Church, Reformed Church in America, United Church of Canada, United Lutheran Church, United Presbyterian Church, *American Friends Service Committee, *Federal Council of the Churches of Christ in America, *National Council of Young Men's Christian Associations, *National Board of Young Women's Christian Associations, *Foreign Missions Conference of North America.

THE STAFF
Toru Matsumoto, *director for resettlement;* Willis G. Hoekje, *associate.*

II

PROTESTANT CHURCH COMMISSION FOR JAPANESE SERVICE

THE CONSTITUENT AGENCIES AND MEMBERSHIP
1942-1945

(Positions refer to the offices held on the Commission)

Northern Baptist: Royal H. Fisher, *chairman,* 3rd year
Congregational and Christian: Clarence S. Gillett
Disciples: Joseph B. Hunter, Galen L. Rose
Evangelical and Reformed: F. J. Schmuck, W. Carl Nugent

Free Methodist-Holiness: Clyde J. Burnett
Friends: Gorman Y. Doubleday
Methodist: Frank Herron Smith, *chairman,* 1st year, John B. Cobb
Presbyterian, U. S. A.: Gordon K. Chapman, *executive secretary*
Protestant Episcopal: Charles S. Reifsnider, *chairman,* 2nd year
American Bible Society: Ralph Bayless
American Friends Service Committee: Joseph Conard, Mrs. J. Duveneck
Student Relocation Council (while the office was in the West): Joseph Conard, H. K. Beale, Denny Wilcher
Salvation Army: Colonel Holland French
Young Men's Christian Associations: Galen M. Fisher
Young Women's Christian Associations: Miss Essie Maguire, Miss Helen Grant
Headquarters of the Commission: 228 McAllister Street, San Francisco 2, California
(The Commission operated as the field agent of the Home Missions Council until the spring of 1945, when it became independent.)

III

HOSTELS

(As of November 1, 1945 *)

Location	*Sponsoring Organizations*
Boston, Massachusetts	Unitarian Service Committee, Congregational Service Committee, and other cooperating committees
Brooklyn, New York	Brethren Service Committee
Buffalo, New York	Buffalo Resettlement Committee
Cincinnati, Ohio	American Friends Service Committee
Cincinnati, Ohio (Family House)	

* There were two hostels in Chicago, through 1943-44, but they were closed earlier than most hostels. Since this list was compiled, many new hostels have been established on the West Coast, totaling more than one hundred, with or without church sponsorship.

Cleveland, Ohio	American Baptist Home Mission Society
Des Moines, Iowa	American Friends Service Committee
Detroit, Michigan	United Ministry to Resettlers, Detroit Council of Churches
Fresno, California	Japanese Methodist Church
Fresno, California	Fresno Buddhist Temple Association
Kansas City, Missouri	Cooperating Protestant, Jewish, and Catholic groups
Los Angeles, California (Evergreen)	Presbyterian Church and American Friends Service Committee
Los Angeles, California (Buddhist)	Buddhist Brotherhood in America
Los Angeles, California	Buddhist Church
Los Angeles, California	Southern California-Arizona Conference of the Methodist Church
Minneapolis, Minnesota	Lutheran Church
Mountain View, California	
New York, New York	Unitarian Service Committee
Oakland, California	National Conference Youth Fellowship (Methodist)
Pasadena, California	American Friends Service Committee
Philadelphia, Pennsylvania	Several cooperating organizations
Rochester, New York	Rochester Resettlement Committee
Sacramento, California	Youth Council of the Methodist Church
Sacramento, California	Japanese American Citizens League
Sacramento, California	Presbyterian Church Council
San José, California	San José Council for Civic Unity
San Francisco, California	Japanese American Sub-Committee of Friends Service Committee of San Francisco
San Francisco, California	Japanese Methodist Church
San Francisco, California	Booker T. Washington Institute
San Francisco, California	President of San Francisco and Protestant Church
San Mateo, California	
Spokane, Washington	American Friends Service Committee and Fellowship Center Committee
Washington, D. C.	Washington Committee for Americans of Japanese Ancestry

THE ASIAN EXPERIENCE
IN NORTH AMERICA

An Arno Press Collection

Andracki, Stanislaw. **Immigration of Orientals into Canada with Special Reference to Chinese.** 1979

Bell, Reginald. **Public School Education of Second-Generation Japanese in California.** 1935

California State Board of Control. **California and the Oriental:** Japanese, Chinese, and Hindus. 1922

Canada, Department of Labour. **Two Reports on Japanese Canadians in World War II.** Two vols. in one. 1944/1947

Canada, Royal Commission on Chinese and Japanese Immigration. **Report of the Royal Commission on Chinese and Japanese Immigration.** 1902

Canada, Royal Commission on Chinese Immigration. **Report of the Royal Commission on Chinese Immigration:** Report and Evidence. 1885

Coman, Katharine. **The History of Contract Labor in the Hawaiian Islands.** 1903 *and* Andrew W[illiam] Lind. **Hawaii's Japanese.** 1946. Two vols. in one

Condit, Ira M. **The Chinaman as We See Him and Fifty Years of Work for Him.** 1900

Conroy, Hilary. **The Japanese Frontier in Hawaii, 1868-1898.** 1953

Daniels, Roger, ed. **Anti-Chinese Violence in North America.** 1979

Daniels, Roger, ed. **Three Short Works on Japanese Americans.** 1979

Daniels, Roger, ed. **Two Monographs on Japanese Canadians.** 1979

Dooner, P[ierton] W. **Last Days of the Republic.** 1880

Flowers, Montaville. **The Japanese Conquest of American Opinion.** 1917

Gibson, O[tis]. **The Chinese in America.** 1877

Gulick, Sidney L[ewis]. **American Democracy and Asiatic Citizenship.** 1918

Hata, Donald Teruo, Jr. **"Undesirables,"** Early Immigrants and the Anti-Japanese Movement in San Francisco, 1892-1893. 1979

Irwin, Wallace. **Seed of the Sun.** 1921

Japan, Consulate General. **Documental History of Law Cases Affecting Japanese in the United States, 1916-1924.** Two vols. in one. 1925

Kachi, Teruko Okada. **The Treaty of 1911 and the Immigration and Alien Land Law Issue Between the United States and Japan, 1911-1913.** 1979

Kawakami, K[iyoshi] K[arl]. **The Real Japanese Question.** 1921

Kyne, Peter B. **The Pride of Palomar.** 1922

LaViolette, Forrest E[manuel]. **Americans of Japanese Ancestry:** A Study of Assimilation in the American Community. 1945

Lee, Rose Hum. **The Growth and Decline of Chinese Communities in the Rocky Mountain Region.** 1979

Li, Tien-Lu. **Congressional Policy of Chinese Immigration:** Or Legislation Relating to Chinese Immigration to the United States. 1916

Matsumoto, Toru. **Beyond Prejudice:** A Story of the Church and Japanese Americans. 1946

McClatchy, Valentine Stuart. **Four Anti-Japanese Pamphlets.** 1979

Mears, Eliot Grinnell. **Resident Orientals on the American Pacific Coast:** Their Legal and Economic Status. 1928

Millis, H. A. **The Japanese Problem in the United States.** 1915

O'Brien, Robert W. **The College Nisei.** 1949

Okubo, Mine. **Citizen 13660.** 1946

Shapiro, H[arry] L[ewis]. **Migration and Environment.** 1939

Steiner, Jesse Frederick. **The Japanese Invasion:** A Study in the Psychology
of Inter-Racial Contacts. 1917

Sugimoto, Howard Hiroshi. **Japanese Immigration, the Vancouver Riots and Canadian Diplomacy.** 1979

Sung, Betty Lee. **Statistical Profile of the Chinese in the United States: 1970 Census.** 1975

Thompson, Richard Austin. The Yellow Peril, 1890-1924. 1979

U. S. House of Representatives, Committee on Immigration and Naturalization. **Japanese Immigration:** Hearings. 1921

U. S. House of Representatives, Select Committee Investigating National Defense Migration. **National Defense Migration:** Hearings. 1942

U. S. Department of State. **Report of the Honorable Roland S. Morris on Japanese Immigration and Alleged Discriminatory Legislation Against Japanese Residents in the U. S.** 1921

U. S. Department of War. **Final Report:** Japanese Evacuation from the West Coast, 1942. 1943

U. S. Senate, Joint Special Committee to Investigate Chinese Immigration. **Report.** 1877

Wing, Yung. **My Life in China and America.** 1909

Wong, Eugene. **On Visual Media Racism:** Asians in the American Motion Pictures. 1979

Wynne, Robert Edward. **Reaction to the Chinese in the Pacific Northwest and British Columbia, 1850-1910.** 1979

Yatsushiro, Toshio. **Politics and Cultural Values:** The World War II Japanese Relocation Centers and the United States Government. 1979

Young, Charles H., Helen R. Y. Reid and W. A. Carrothers. **The Japanese Canadians.** 1938

Zo, Kil Young. **Chinese Emigration into the United States, 1850-1880.** 1979